CW00922297

The
VERSATILE
PRESENTER

Master **12** styles

get the response you need

Richard Pascoe

Kirstie Hawkes

The
CONTENTS

Praise for the Book

Geraldine Huse

President Procter & Gamble Canada

"This book is amazing! You can just dip into it to find a new tip which will give you confidence for your next big moment... Whether you are speaking at your employee's retirement dinner or at a massive conference of seasoned professionals, this book has the tips and tricks to help you perform even better than you hoped."

James Mills

Global VP of Sales. Mars Inc.

"As a salesperson for most of my professional life I wish someone had told me a long time ago that I needed to unfix myself from the "always-be-selling" mindset in presentations. Let this book help you put the audience at the heart of your communication."

Chantal Cornelius

National President of the Professional Speaking Association (PSA UK) 2023–2024 and Speaker at Appletree Marketing

"What makes this book different to the myriad other books on presentation skills? It guides you to work out exactly why you're giving your next presentation, what outcome you want for your audience and helps you choose the most appropriate type of presentation. Too many presenters lack this essential focus and don't, therefore, leave the lasting impact that they want to make. After all, isn't that what we all want, as speakers?"

Francesco Mantovani

Procter & Gamble Global Learning Technologies and Innovation Leader

"This book is a step-by-step guide on how to mesmerize different audiences! When presenting, different situations and audiences each require a specific approach; this book is an amazingly easy-to-apply guide to smash any presentation using the proper words, tone, visuals, body language and tactics."

Chantal Taylor

Group Head of HR, TTP

"Playful and practical. Read this to inject personality into your presentations!"

More praise for the book on page 244

Get the **Most** Out of this Book

We suggest you do the following:

#1 Download the free one-page summary of the twelve prez-types.

Use this QR code or go straight to:

www.versatilepresenter.com/resources

You will find other extra materials and templates here too.

#2 Have a real presentation to consider.

People have told us that they find the book most valuable when they have a real presentation in mind as they read. Especially as they explored the "DO IT" section of the book for the first time. If you have a presentation coming up, or can imagine one that makes sense to you, use this as the test case as you read.

#3 Read Part 1: "The IDEA" and Part 2: "The PREZ METHOD" to get familiar with the approach.

This is a "How-to" book. Part 3: "DO IT" (half of the book) is made up of twelve reference chapters, each full of tips on a specific presenter type. The final two parts of the book are designed to answer further questions and offer you more content if you are interested.

PART 1 (12 pages)	PART 2 (42 pages)	PART 3 (146 pages)	PART 4 (28 pages)	PART 5 (10 pages)
The IDEA	The PREZ METHOD	DO IT	GOING FURTHER	MORE?

You may enjoy going deep into certain sections OR you may prefer to skip past some. Look out for this icon. This tells you that the next section is designed for anyone who wants to go deeper, but there is no harm in jumping forward.

Finally: Keep this book on your desk, and every time you have a presentation coming up, grab it.

Foreword 1: **by Paul Smith**

Bestselling Author and Professional Keynote Speaker

This book is based on a novel, perhaps even shocking, concept: you need not – in fact you *should* not – have the same style of presenting every time you do so.

I've been delivering corporate presentations for over thirty years, and been a professional keynote speaker and trainer for a dozen of those. So I'm constantly trying to improve the effectiveness of my presentations and speaking style. Which means that I'm frequently adding and subtracting things from my personal process. But it never occurred to me, until now, that there wasn't just one best way for me to do what I do.

When I'm on stage delivering a keynote address about storytelling (my particular area of expertise), I'm the expert expounding on my years of study and experience, trying to impart as much knowledge as I can in the time allotted. But when I'm on a phone call with a prospective client, I'm a salesman and the product I'm selling is me. When I'm sharing preliminary results of new research at the local university, I'm a student looking to learn as much as I am teaching.

In all these situations, my presentation style was always the same, because I only knew one way to do it. The ideas in this book opened my eyes to an alternative I hadn't considered. Maybe a different style would be more effective in different situations. And apparently that can be done without diminishing my authenticity or making me somehow less genuine.

In this book, Richard and Kirstie take you through a straightforward four-step process, 'The Prez Method', to customise any presentation to the situation.

The Prez Method starts with determining your intent or objective of the presentation. Are you trying to teach something? Inspire change? Motivate a specific behaviour? Given that, you choose from a dozen different types of presenter you want to be – each of these twelve connecting back to archetypes based on the work by psychologist Carl Jung.

Once you know that, you can alter the design of your presentation materials (your message) and the style of your delivery (word choice, body language, visuals, and your attitude!) to match that intent and type.

I've known and worked with Richard for almost twenty years, as both a colleague and a student in his classes. In partnership with Kirstie Hawkes, there is no one better equipped to teach this topic.

Paul Smith – Bestselling author of *Sell with a Story* and *The 10 Stories Great Leaders Tell*.

> *Richard adds:*
>
> **Paul Smith: writer of some of the best books on real business stories and how to tell them.**

Foreword 2: **by Stewart Lee**

BAFTA Winning Stand-up Comedian and Writer

I am a stand-up comedian, and like Kirstie Hawkes and Richard Pascoe, who have co-authored *The Versatile Presenter*, I make a living out of standing up and presenting ideas to strangers. And the book addresses the same professional problems I encounter, but it solves them calmly and rationally, rather than with alcohol, late nights, and crying.

It's not strange that Kirstie and I should work in tangentially similar fields, as it turns out she is my half-sister, but I only met her for the first time eleven years ago. But since 2006, Kirstie had been showing clients a film of me satirising marketing in the BBC TV series *Time Trumpet*, without knowing we were siblings. It's strange to think that Kirstie, Richard and I were already working together without realising it.

As I write this foreword, about two months behind schedule on creating a new live show, the pair's opening section talks directly to me. "*Petrified by the blank page,*" they write, "*What should the message be? What content should you include (and exclude)? What sort of story or structure should you use?*" And then, "*Bound to one presentation performance style? How do you release yourself from your habitual communicating style to present in one of a variety of styles? This book is going to unfix you. It will give you the ideas, the method, and the tools to become a truly versatile presenter.*" It seems the universe gives you the sister, and the sister's friend, you need.

The book's central thrust concerns adopting personae in business presentations. I do this too – usually entering into exaggerated versions of my worst self – and it's a problem-solving strategy I recognise. Once the American wrestler Colt Cabana told me I was playing both 'The Face' (hero) and 'The Heel' (villain) simultaneously, which was news to me, but probably not to the authors of *The Versatile Presenter*. I think all of us have a foothold in *The Versatile Presenter*'s way of thinking, whether we are aware of it or not.

Gliding admirably between high culture and low culture without judgement, seeking reflections of Jung's archetypes in sources as diverse as Mr Miyagi's *Karate Kid* antics, Bill Mantlo's Rocket Racoon from Marvel comics' *Guardians of The Galaxy*, and Mhairi Black's SNP speeches, *The Versatile Presenter* will make a business presentation guru of me yet.

Stewart Lee –Writer/clown, Stoke Newington, August 2024

Kirstie adds:

Stewart Lee: Pioneer of British comedy; British Comedy Awards, Olivier Awards and BAFTA winner... and top-notch brother since 2013.

1

The
IDEA

You can flex to **any presentation** situation.

You set the **audience response you need**...

...and select an **ideal type of presenter**...

...to sharpen the **design of your presentation**...

...and to shift your **style of delivery**.

The Core of this Book

Presenters Stuck in the Middle

This book is written for any professional who can honestly say they are **already a good presenter**: someone with significant experience in making presentations at work. Someone who has circumnavigated the normal presentation pitfalls; someone who **now needs to be a great presenter in multiple scenarios**.

You may present to a small team or you may present to an entire organisation. You may present as a functional support in a project team or as the owner of the whole business. You may present brands, clients, customers, systems, processes, infrastructures, projects, or other things. You are neither starting out nor closing out your career. You are somewhere in the middle.

And you may feel, in some way, stuck!

Perhaps you feel **stuck being a 'good presenter'** but you want to be a 'great presenter'. Perhaps you feel **stuck in a rut, presenting in a similar way** every time, which limits your ability to get to the outcomes that you need. Perhaps you feel **stuck in your career** and want a way to be seen as a more complete leader.

You Need to Unfix to Flex

We can all feel constrained as we present. We can be overwhelmed by a quagmire of questions:

1) **Glued to too many outcomes:** Which outcomes are most important? How can you set a precise objective for a presentation with so many consequences riding on it? How can you select an appropriate sort of presentation to deliver?

2) **Petrified by the blank page:** What should the message be? What content should you include (and exclude)? What sort of story or structure should you use?

3) **Bound to one presentation performance style:** How do you release yourself from your habitual style of presentation? How do you find other ways to present? How do you stay authentically you as you do so?

This book is going to 'unfix' you. It will give you the ideas, the method, and the tools to break away from your one way of presenting and free you to become a truly versatile presenter.

An Established Idea in a **New Method**

The ideas in this book are Established

At the heart of this book is the solidity and security of archetypes: Carl Jung's explanation of the 'collective unconscious' found in all of us.[01]

In today's working world, archetypes are the bedrock of valuable business models. For example: personality profiles to help managers understand their working style;[02] marketing communications theory to help develop a unique and consistent equity.[03]

Archetypes are also found regularly within the creative arts: archetypes help screenwriters to craft distinct characters;[04] archetypes help actors to morph into varied believable performances.[05]

The ideas in this book are Unique

We have written this book because no one else seems to have done so. The underlying ideas are longstanding, but we believe it is new to harness these within the context of business presentations.

This brings fresh thinking to how to plan and deliver presentations. This includes two perspectives: firstly, we make the obvious yet empowering step to bring archetype principles into presentation skills; and secondly, we add a vast catalogue of practical tips and techniques to help you to execute these ideas.

Designed for Many **Real Business Scenarios**

We have read a great number of presentation skills books. We admire many. We recommend some. However, there is a trend for the books to be too focussed on one of the following:

✕ *"One size fits all."* ✕

These books over-simplify for your needs. They offer useful advice on things like managing nerves. However, they distil everything down into overly general principles like *"No more than three bullet points on every slide"*. There is no nuance to the different situations you present in.

✕ *"Your objective is always to persuade."* ✕

These are often books written by ex-salespeople.[06] They tend to overemphasise the importance of persuasion. The 'always-be-selling' approach is valid in some limited scenarios, but in a business career you need to do many more things beyond selling ideas.

Designed For **Fast OR Slow**

The reality of the working world means how long you have to design a presentation can vary significantly. Sometimes the presentation is sufficiently important that you have a few weeks to deliberate over each element of its content and design. Sometimes (in our experience, often) the presentation is tomorrow and you need to make fast decisions.

> This book will introduce you to our process: **The Prez Method** ™

The Prez Method has four steps. These will be explained in detail in Part 2, but in essence...

These four steps: **Set, Select, Sharpen,** and **Shift,** are designed so you can use them slowly and deliberately (we call this 'tortoise-speed') or you can use them quickly and simply (we call this 'hare-speed'):

At tortoise-speed:

Say that you have two weeks to prepare your presentation.

You work systematically through each of the four steps of **The Prez Method.** The method supports every decision you make on your presentation, including: your messaging, content, slide design, language, staging, visuals, and more.

At hare-speed:

Say that you have two hours to prepare your presentation.

You work at speed. You only have time to make a few fast decisions. The four steps help you quickly make strategic choices. This gives your presentation the right tone and style of delivery.

What Do We Mean by a **"Presentation"?**

A presentation is any situation where you are sharing prepared information with an audience for a purpose that you can define. It can be delivered live or pre-recorded. It can be to one person or to over 100 people. It can be two minutes or two hours long. It can be delivered with everyone in a single room, or with people in different locations (e.g. virtual).

That's the idea and that's what it offers you. Now, to trust the idea, it can help to know the origin of the idea.

The Origin **Story**

OK to jump

Richard as Peter Snow or Gandalf

It is 2001. The first of the *Lord of the Rings* trilogy of films, directed by Peter Jackson, is in cinemas.[07] Mobile phones are yet to become "smart". And I am 25 years old and working at Procter & Gamble as a market and sales analyst. I spend my days analysing sales and research data to better understand what shoppers are buying (and what we might do to get them to buy more).

In my role, I regularly present to the team; normally updates on market trends. I am known in the office as a charismatic and energetic presenter. It helps that I am naturally fascinated by the information that I share and I know how to keep data decks interactive and entertaining. I also don't take myself too seriously – happy to poke fun at my ignorance.

I am flattered when, on a few occasions, people from the audience come to me afterwards to compare my presenting style to Peter

Snow. Peter Snow is a well-known face on UK television.[08] He presents iconic BBC programmes like *Tomorrow's World* and *Newsnight*. He is the face and voice of election data. Every general election since 1966 has seen Peter Snow presenting the voting results as each count comes in. He is enthralled by the data, enthusiastic to share the data stories that appear, and he is modest about his own expertise.

I feel very proud that people compare my presenting style to him. This fills me with confidence.

Then I hit a problem.

Increasingly, the team need me to present at important external client meetings. I set the context and data landscape for the ideas they will pitch to the client. Sitting in these meetings I feel very aware how much younger I am than many around me. Suddenly my confident 'Peter Snow-like' style feels chaotic, unprofessional and, perhaps, immature.

This is how I present. I do not know how to adapt my style to different scenarios. I cannot find any book that offers a solution. I am good at presenting and yet not good at presenting. I feel stuck.

Around this time, like millions of others, I visit the cinema to see the first *Lord of the Rings* film. I am transfixed by Gandalf. The wizard is confident, experienced, credible and wise, while still having moments of enthusiasm and fun. Exactly as I wish I could come across. I have an idea.

Maybe I can choose to be 'Gandalf-like'. Not to the majestic level of Ian McKellen (who could?), but enough to add gravitas to how I speak. It might be a trick to unstick my style of presenting?

At the next external presentation, to an Asda buying team, I give this a go. As I begin to speak, I tell myself that "I am Gandalf". Every time my Peter Snow starts to materialise, I remind myself that "I am Gandalf". As I close my presentation, summarising the most important points, I confirm to myself that "I am Gandalf".

I find this makes a transformative yet subtle difference to how I come across. I talk more slowly. I pause more confidently. I speak with a higher level of assuredness. I am more comfortable sharing my 'expert' opinion. I am less keen to please. I am more credible.

By giving myself this internal statement of self-identity, my subconscious takes over and I know how to speak.

I am still Richard presenting as Richard. The audience sees an authentic version of me. But now it is a version of me with greater authority, calmer, more thoughtful, and more impressive.

I am elated. I am unstuck!

Over the coming weeks, in various presentations, I continue to experiment with this idea. I do not let go of my original style – at times I want that more innocent and modest style that Peter Snow offers me. But when I want people to listen intently to my opinion (rather than be guided through complex facts), I switch on Gandalf.

A few months later an Asda Head Office contact calls me with a favour: they have been asked to deliver a presentation at a big industry conference in Madrid, but they cannot make it. Would I, possibly, consider speaking on their behalf?

I have gone from being a great presenter in limited situations (internal data presentations with my team) to a great presenter in more situations (adding external analysis presentations to give expert opinions).

In the coming years, I become the first Global Course Owner for the *'Inspirational Presenter Course'*. Procter & Gamble sees me as their internal global expert in advanced presentation skills. I literally write, with Kirstie, their book on how to train advanced presentation skills to their leaders across the world.

The more people we train, the more we find others with the same challenge that I had early in my career. People stuck in their version of Peter Snow. Presenting well in some situations, but unable to adapt to others.

Kirstie and I slowly form a method to help anyone become a more versatile presenter. How does this method help?

How This Book Will **Help You**

This Book Is For You If:

You are a good presenter, and in some situations a great one, <u>but</u> too often you struggle to get the results that you want. ☐ YES

You have a style of presenting that you know well, <u>but</u> you rely too much on this one way. ☐ YES

You have delivered many presentations <u>yet</u> you are still affected by your fear of failing to speak well. ☐ YES

You know some good ways of structuring your presentation, <u>but</u> you want more structures to choose from. ☐ YES

You deliver effective presentations, <u>but</u> you want to be more expressive and engaging. ☐ YES

Learn From Our Experience

We have worked in marketing, sales, insights, external relations, and consulting. We have made thousands of business presentations.

We have been using **The Prez Method** with leaders across all levels and multiple countries for over ten years.

We work with huge multinationals like Procter & Gamble and Carlsberg. We work with third sector charities like Trussell Trust and Switchback.

You Will **Set** a Presentation Intention

You know you are supposed to define a clear objective for your presentation, but what does that really mean?

You will learn to analyse each presentation in relation to four types of desired audience response: knowledge, change, **belonging**, or actions. You will learn to place these presentation intentions ('**prez-intents**') around a circle (like poles around a compass). This will give you exceptional clarity in what you are trying to achieve – a direction to focus on.

You Will **Select** a Type of Presentation

You realise you should design the presentation to meet this prez-intent, but how?

You will select a type of presentation to be the seed for key decisions. Your prez-intent leads you to a collection of types of presentation ('**prez-types**') to pick from. Perhaps a choice between 'hero' or 'magician' or between 'ruler', 'creator', or 'student'. From these, you select the prez-type that best fits you as a person, your content, and your audience. It can be that easy.

You set the **strategy for your presentation: your prez-intent and your prez-type.** Now you move to execution.

You Will **Sharpen** Your Presentation Design

How will the prez-type help you craft your presentation?

The prez-type will guide how you sculpt all aspects of your presentation. This will include: the type of messaging, content prioritisation, the structure and flow, the ways in which you interact with your audience, and more.

When the work to design the presentation has only just begun, you can use these as blueprints to carefully follow.

When the presentation design is mostly ready, you can use these as a toolbox of useful ideas for quick inspiration; tips to make fast final improvements.

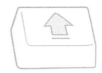

You Will **Shift** Your Style Intuitively

How will the prez-type transform your delivery?

We have all heard the truism, *"It is not what you say but how you say it."* The Prez Method will show you how to flex your style so *'how you say it'* best fits with *'what you say'*.

You will be amazed at how quickly and intuitively you can do this. For example, if you choose to be an explorer prez-type, you can focus on being adventurous in style. Telling yourself, *"I am an explorer"* will give you the essence of exploration.

You will find in this book an abundance of tips, tricks, suggestions, thoughts, and hints for each prez-type. Skimming over a few pages will be enough to fill your mind with creative and practical ideas.

A Summary Of How **This Book Helps**

O By reading this book you will get tortoise-paced and hare-paced ways to become a more versatile presenter.

O By learning the core of **The Prez Method** you will develop the skills to become a more versatile presenter.

O By keeping this book nearby you will benefit from a reference source of tips and techniques to unstick each of your presentations.

We are promising a lot. You may have some reasonable doubts. Here's a real-world story to allay those fears.
Let us introduce Jamie, a director at SPAR UK.

The Example **Story**

Jamie as Determined Hero

Jamie is the brand director for SPAR UK,[09] making him the custodian of the SPAR brand (SPAR own label lines) across more than 2,000 convenience stores in the UK.

In March 2024, Jamie delivered a presentation to over 500 colleagues, store owners, and suppliers. Jamie's priority was to inspire everyone to see the growth of the SPAR brand as being integral to the long-term strategy for the business.

Jamie worked with Richard and Kirstie, using **The Prez Method**:

Jamie: *"It helped take me out of daily slide building and really think about my purpose: Why were the audience there? What could motivate them? And how could I tailor my message to both hit their needs and my own strategic needs for the business?"*

Jamie's prez-intent was change: to transform his audience's perception of SPAR brand. **The Prez Method** gave him a choice of four types of presenter: **hero, magician, explorer,** and **maverick.** These key factors made the selection relatively clear:

- Other convenience retailers were struggling to keep their own label brands a viable part of their business.

- Jamie wanted the store owners to roll up their sleeves and get involved – to feel emboldened to act.

- Failing to strengthen and grow the SPAR brand could undermine the business's ability to grow in the future.

Jamie selected the **hero prez-type.** Driving growth for the SPAR brand was a vital endeavour. There would be short-term challenges, but the dangers of inaction (not supporting) meant it was important to tackle the challenges head-on.

This gave Jamie the creative seed he needed to build the final presentation. It also gave him the way to shift his delivery into a style full of vital purpose and bravery.

Below is a short excerpt from the <u>end</u> of Jamie's presentation. Just from these words we get a sense of how Jamie brought the essence of hero into his final messages.

The following is Jamie's original script. It is the final few minutes of his presentation. We have abridged some elements.

His language is peppered with language of the **hero-type** presenter.

"Not being successful on this mission is not an option. Together, over decades, we've built this brand and collectively we can ensure its success. But it won't 'just happen'…

"…We are laser focussed on bringing you great tasting, great value products, so that you can wow your shoppers with value, choice and quality.

"We need to maximise what we have, and bring new products in – and you have a huge role to play in both.

"It's our collective job – and my personal mission – to ensure that SPAR brand is an invaluable asset for your business for generations to come. Join me on this mission, and we'll go places.

"And so, my plea to you all is to 'switch ON' your passion and your action, to make a difference in your stores.

"Your SPAR brand products are exclusively available in SPAR stores. SPAR was the first to play in this space, and we're just about the last. But we're not just surviving, we're thriving. And that's down to you, Winning with Product by supporting the brand that's above your door."

The results? Here is how Jamie summarised it:

"The audience response was just what I wanted. The feedback on the day and retrospectively has been extremely positive. And we've seen an increase in our sales and participation since the event."

Two Important **Cornerstones**

We have already given you a lot to mull over. Let us close Part 1: THE IDEA by highlighting two important cornerstones for this book. To do this we will talk about a tennis player and a piano player.

Cornerstone 1: **You Need Multiple Ways to Present**
or: **A Superb Serve Won't Win You the French Open**

Imagine that you are a young and aspiring tennis player. Your game is based on a superb serve. The shot is a thing of beauty; consistently the ball kisses the white lines as you hit ace after ace. You can hit a pretty good topspin forehand and own a respectable backhand slice. But your great strength is that superb serve.

This serve will get you a good way through the amateur leagues of tennis. But you have ambitions to become a top professional tennis player. Your exceptional serve will bring some success at Wimbledon – a server's paradise – but life will soon be tough for you on the clay courts at the French Open. Your superb serve will sit up for your opponent to smash past you a winning return. One type of shot is not enough. You are going to need to be a more versatile tennis player.

To be clear, your game is going to continue to be built around your greatest strength: that superb serve. But to develop a 'complete game' you need to excel at a range of shots. Your topspin forehand and backhand slice need to be great too.

Being a 'world-class' tennis player is <u>not</u> about being the best at all of the shots; it is about having sufficient high-level shot options to excel on any court surface and against any player. If you only have one great type of shot, you will only win tennis matches on some surfaces and against limited opposition.

As a versatile presenter, you do not need to be a jedi master of every type of presentation, but if you only master one way of speaking, you are limiting your ability to make an impact in many business situations. You need to be able to deliver different types of presentation on different occasions to different audiences.

Now, let's talk about the piano...

Cornerstone 2: Subtle Changes Make a Huge Difference
or: 88 Piano Keys, Profoundly Diverse Music

You probably remember someone from your school days who was a good piano player. Perhaps they entertained everyone at every party with covers of Beatles classics. They could play all the notes on the piano with consummate skill.

Now imagine that friend being a professional piano player. Their career is as a professional pianist.

What does that really mean? While a pianist may be playing a piano of eighty-eight piano keys, their objective, their raison d'être, will vary considerably based on the musical scenario.

One week they may be a classical concert pianist. Their role is to be the primary star of the musical performance. They strive to enthral the audience with their musical virtuosity.

The next week they may be a répétiteur (rehearsal pianist) for a stage musical. They need to stick rigidly to the music laid down by the composer. They need to know when to help the singer (e.g. bring the tune out in the accompaniment) and when to balance with the singer (step away from the tune and add richness in the harmonies).

The final week they may be a keyboard player in a jazz quartet. There is no sheet music to follow, instead there is an agreed tune and chord sequence. They need to improvise in an ever-evolving conversation with the other musicians.

Each week, our piano player is playing the same set of eighty-eight piano keys with the same two hands. The skill of the true professional is to vary how they play those eighty-eight piano keys, based on the type of music they are playing and the musical scenario they are in.

As a versatile presenter, you need to be equally as skilled at making subtle changes in how you use messages, stories, gestures, audience interaction and more. You are using the same 'presentation keys' to deliver profoundly different presentations.

Moving On...
That closes off Part 1: The IDEA. Next we get to learn about each step of **The Prez Method** in detail.

2 The PREZ METHOD

An Overview

The Prez Method is a four-step process:

1) **SET** the prez-intent (the intent of your presentation): the audience response you want

2) **SELECT** your prez-type (presenter type) that will support your prez-intent

3) **SHARPEN** your prez-content: the design of your presentation

4) **SHIFT** your prez-style: how you deliver your presentation, influenced by your prez-type

At first glance, this looks simple enough. However, even with so few steps, it is easy to feel lost when you are within it.

It will help you if, from the start, you see **The Prez Method** as split into two parts. Firstly, you decide on what you are trying to achieve from your presentation and, secondly, you work out how you will present. It is strategy first and execution second.

Strategy Precedes Execution

A) STRATEGY (Planning)

What you are intending to achieve from your presentation and the type of presentation you will use.

B) EXECUTION (Creating)

How you will bring this type of presentation to life through messaging, structure, language, visuals, etc.

SET   SELECT

SHARPEN   SHIFT

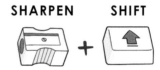

This feels like a sensible way to do things. We can all relate to the need to make the higher-level decisions on why and what before we get into the weeds of how, where, and when. More specifically you will:

Make good choices on what you want to achieve from your presentation ("**SET**") and what type of presenter you will centre your presentation around ("**SELECT**").

Use the type of presenter you chose to tailor your presentation design ("**SHARPEN**") and to embody the type of presenter ("**SHIFT**").

That gives you the bird's eye view of the method. Next we drop down a level to where we can see more detail on the four steps.

The Prez Method: Process Steps

Here is a brief summary of what you do for each step of the method.

STRATEGY

1 SET YOUR PREZ-INTENT

2 SELECT YOUR PREZ-TYPE

Define the response that you want from your audience. You set the intent of your presentation (your **prez-intent**).

Consider **four prez-intents**:

1. Expand their **Knowledge**

2. Inspire gut-feel to **Change**

3. Develop sense of **Belonging**

4. Direct their **Actions**

Lay out the four prez-intents as cardinal poles.
Set your direction:

Choose a **prez-type** (presenter type) that will support your **prez-intent**.

There are **twelve prez-types**:

Hero			Magician
Explorer			Maverick
Sage			Jester
Student			Lover
Creator			Everyman
Ruler			Caregiver

Your **prez-intent** will guide you on which **prez-type** to choose.

EXECUTION

3 SHARPEN
YOUR
PREZ-CONTENT

4 SHIFT
YOUR
PREZ-STYLE

Use the **prez-type** to lead your hand as you craft the details of your presentation.

Use the **prez-type** to:

○ hone your messaging – your precise language and meaning.

○ shave your info – prioritise and deprioritise content to include.

○ chart your structure – arrangement and sequence of your content.

Allow the **prez-type** to transform how you deliver your presentation.

Let the **prez-type** inspire:

○ the language you use.

○ your body language.

○ how you move around the space.

○ your use of visuals.

○ how to manage notes.

○ how to interact with the audience.

At tortoise-speed:

When you have time to invest, **The Prez Method** can be undertaken methodically. Steps 1 and 2 (SET and SELECT) are made at the very start of the development process. **Every aspect of your presentation is inspired by the prez-type selected.**

At hare-speed:

When time is tight, each step can enable small tweaks that you make soon before you present. **Final choices and subtle shifts in delivery can be inspired by the prez-type selected.**

Here is a simplified example.

STRATEGY

1 SET YOUR PREZ-INTENT

2 SELECT YOUR PREZ-TYPE

Carl is the operations leader at a company that designs and manufactures heat pumps for home heating.

Carl needs to present to his team, asking them each to complete a report summarising installation issues from the last twelve months.

In simple terms, he wants them all to complete a series of steps after the presentation.

Carl draws a crude sketch of the four **prez-intents**.

Carl sets his **prez-intent** as: Actions.

Carl reviews the four **prez-types** that are found around **Actions**.

creator, ruler, caregiver, everyman

creator, ruler, caregiver, and **everyman**

Carl considers his preferred styles, what the audience needs, and the content he needs to share with them.

Carl selects **caregiver prez-type** because:

1) he can frame the request as protecting them from annoying exec team questions.

2) he feels comfortable that this prez-type fits well with his personal style.

EXECUTION

3 SHARPEN YOUR PREZ-CONTENT

4 SHIFT YOUR PREZ-STYLE

Carl does not have the time to labour over this presentation. He needs to pull together something quickly. He grabs this book and jumps straight to the chapter on the **caregiver prez-type**.

Carl forms a main message – aiming for something that is a "guidance". *"Let me help you get your installation concerns voiced to the executive."*

Next Carl chooses what content to cover. Again, the **caregiver** chapter helps him make choices. He prioritises:

- ◯ **Expectations:** clarify what they could look to share.

- ◯ **Guardrails:** reassurances that they can safely share their real feedback with leadership.

- ◯ **Guidelines:** outline how the report should be completed.

As Carl steps up to present, he consciously chooses to shift his style into **caregiver**. He emphasises that he is here to assist them, *"Team, our executive are reviewing the results this year and making big choices about next year. You want them making choices with knowledge of the real issues you are facing in your installations. My job today is to guide you through the process that we will all follow so that you get your concerns voiced to the executive."*

Carl intuitively speaks more slowly and calmly. He keeps his language simple and easy to understand.

Carl's audience responds instinctively: they listen carefully (because it is about their safety), and they focus on the steps to be taken (following Carl's guidance). The team start writing their reports within days of the meeting.

Next we look at each of these steps in more detail, explaining more fully how **The Prez Method** works.

SET

In Summary

Step 1:
SET Your Prez-intent:

You have an objective for your presentation. You must transform this into a statement of intention – what you want your audience to do.

You are considering four primary prez-intents: knowledge, change, **belonging**, and **actions**.

These four prez-intents sit at the cardinal points around a compass.

You **SET your prez-intent** by marking a direction with an arrow.

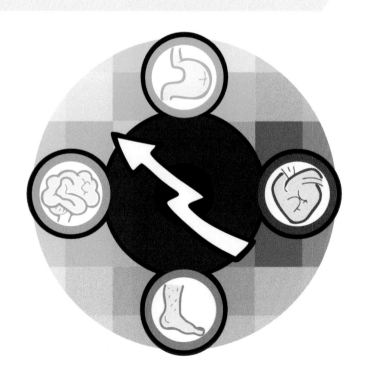

Step 1: SET Your Prez-intent

Turn Objective into Outcome

There needs to be a reason for your presentation – an objective that you have. However, an objective on its own is a fairly useless thing as you prepare and deliver your real presentation.

Imagine you are playing a game of tennis. The ball is flying towards you. Telling yourself that your objective is "to win the point" is not a lot of use. Your arms and legs know little about how to move and how to hit the ball as you want.

You need to set an outcome for that shot – *"pass him down the line."* You may miss the tramline, but at least your brain and your arms and your legs all knew what they were trying to do individually and in combination.

In a presentation the sensation can be similar. With everything going on, as you stand and talk to your audience, having a broad objective only gets you so far. If you choose that you want to *"deploy the initiative"*, it is like saying to yourself *"I want to win the point."* You don't know how to say things, how to use your body language, how to move around the space as you present.

You need to transform your objective into an outcome that you want – and this will be a response that you want from your audience.

"The impact of your presentation is your audience's response."
Paul Z Jackson [10]

Rather than the objective of *"deploy the initiative to the sales team"* you describe the response that you want. Perhaps: *"Get the sales teams to pitch the initiative brilliantly to their major clients within two months."*

Better! But does this really give you enough information to know how to craft your words and convey your meaning?

Turn Outcome into Intent

You need to bring your desired outcome back into a simple intent: what you are endeavouring to do as you communicate.

Consider the tennis shot again. Set a true intent for the shot: *"Hit a fast topspin shot to land just inside the tramlines."* Now your legs know how to move, and your arms know how to swing your racket.

For any presentation, you set a simple intent, a 'prez-intent': what you are focussed on doing as you present, e.g. *"Challenge the sales teams to pitch the initiative the best they can."*

Your first step is to set the intent of your presentation, to **SET your prez-intent**.

To help you do this, you consider four primary directions of prez-intent. Four distinct ways you may want your audience to listen and to respond.

Four Prez-intents to Choose from

There are any number of ways that you may want your audience to respond to your presentation. Picking from a plethora of options can feel overwhelming, and is likely to lead most of us to drop our pencil and go off for a coffee break. To help you choose, you simplify your considerations down to four prez-intents; four ways in which your audience may respond.

Four Prez-intents

Expand their
Knowledge

> You want your audience to increase their understanding in a topic.

Inspire gut-feel
to **Change**

> You want your audience to change their viewpoint or perspective.

Develop sense
of **Belonging**

> You want your audience to feel trust in you, themselves, or the team.

Direct their
Actions

> You want your audience to complete a sequence of steps or actions.

Why These Four Prez-intents?

They work and they help.

They generalise the sort of objective that you have in a work presentation, and they focus you into one of four types of response that you want from your audience.

When you want to impart important information, it makes you focus on growing their knowledge and understanding. When you want to turn a "probably no" into a "probably yes", it makes you focus on changing their point of view. When you want to build team spirit, it makes you focus on developing their sense of belonging and trust. If you want to brief them to complete a sequence of next steps, it makes you focus on directing their actions.

In short, it moves you from an objective, through an outcome, all the way to a prez-intent.

Do They Cover All Situations?

Probably not. No model is perfect.

At the same time, we have yet to come across a situation that cannot be described through the language of these four prez-intents.

Why Not Be More Specific in Your Prez-intent?

You likely have something more specific in mind for the outcome of your presentation. For example, if you are presenting to your vice president (Maria), it might be: *"Gain buy-in from Maria to add £100,000 to the agency budget for the delivery of Project Alaska."* You have a definitive goal.

This specificity helps you make intellectual choices on content, but it does not help you adapt your style as you prepare and deliver your presentation. **You want a direction of intent rather than just the destination.** Presenting can feel like bobbing up and down in a small sailing boat in the middle of a large sea. You can decide to sail to the nearest harbour, but this is nothing more than a dream until you have a bearing to follow.

Your prez-intent is your presentation direction of travel.

Just as you can travel north, east, south or west, your intent can be aimed towards change (north), belonging (east), actions (south), or knowledge (west).

Consider How You Want Your Audience to Think

Moreover, the four prez-intents articulate something important about how your audience will think. You want your audience to be **listening in the right way to the content you share.**

I should not expect my audience to listen to learn... and listen to reconsider... and listen to connect... and listen to commit to instructions **all at the same time.** Yet, we do this all the time in business presentations. The result is our audience wastes thinking time and focusses on ascertaining what the presenter is trying to achieve.[11] The audience wants to know what the presenter is trying to convey and what the presenter is really asking of them.

By setting a singular primary prez-intent you can then make choices that will help your audience to sit and be attentive to the right elements of your presentation.

Let's consider each prez-intent and how we want our audience to listen.

We guide our audience to listen in the right way.

Inspire gut-feel to **Change**

They listen to reconsider.
They question their existing beliefs. They compare your promises to how they see the world. They ask you questions in order to confirm they have it right.

Expand their **Knowledge**

They listen to learn.
They look to connect ideas to their existing understanding. They think deeply about the details. They ask questions in order to check they understand the information correctly.

Develop sense of **Belonging**

They listen to trust you and each other. They look to build friendships. They become comfortable with the "norms of this tribe". They ask questions in order to meet, connect, and play.

Direct their **Actions**

They listen to follow.
They note process steps. They focus on details about work for them to complete. They ask questions in order to check they have the expectations and targets.

So I Pick One of the Four Prez-intents?

Not quite. Instead, you set a direction. You can consider the circle as a compass, and you plot a bearing. You can head directly towards one of the cardinal points; or you can set a direction between two, offering you more flexibility.

If you only need to shift their thinking on a topic (**change**), you draw your arrow straight up.

If you mostly have information they need to understand (**knowledge**) but also have a process to brief them (**actions**), you might draw this.

If you want your audience to feel equally confident in you (**belonging**) as they are clear on the steps they should take (**actions**), you draw between the two.

Alexander is preparing a presentation to the leadership team who are visiting his office to review progress and priorities.

The key results from his team look good, but Alexander wants the leadership team to see past the short-term successes and realise the good times won't last much longer. He notes down his intent: "I need to get the lead team to look at the business with fresh eyes. And I need to help them understand the recent market data."

Alexander draws his prez-intent arrow equally between **change** and **knowledge.**

This Comes with Experience

In time, you may set more than one prez-intent for some presentations. For now, as we walk you through **The Prez Method**, we will focus on presentations where you can set a single prez-intent. Where you head in one direction. Later in the book, in Part 4: GOING FURTHER, we give tips on more complicated presentations. For now, we set a single prez-intent. What next?

OK to jump

Tell Me More: Scenarios for Each Prez-intent

Knowledge **Scenarios:**

We all need to know things. Your audience navigates through their lives by accessing knowledge. They succeed through mastering principles, models, data, and facts. They rely on established information but are intrigued by the new and cutting-edge developments.

For example: *Leadership have aligned on a new set of priorities for the next twelve months. They need to understand the implications of these priorities on the supply chain. Rina needs to explain how the choices may create short-term supply issues (partly because of a delay on "switching-on" the latest warehousing consolidation). She wants to focus her information on the four factories that will need to make significant changes to production capacity.*

In other "knowledge" examples, you may need to:

O Share the new consumer and market analysis and trends. To help your audience comprehend the business opportunities available.

O Summarise established and latest thinking on product design. To take your audience through key information so they have a firm overview of what is known.

O Update them on a project's progress. To clarify to the audience the present situation, where things are on track, and where there are concerns.

Change **Scenarios:**

When we change our perspective, we talk about feeling it in our gut – it is a visceral sensation. To persuade an audience that change is needed, we need them to feel an instinctive sense that a fresh perspective is justified and practical. Rationality will be important, but only once you have convinced them something needs to change. To start a change that change needs to feel right.

For example: *Hana is invited to speak to the leadership team to update them on her lead project. They are expecting a general summary of progress, but she is recommending a significant strategy change: more ambitious goals but over a longer time frame. This will involve everyone shifting their expectations on what can be delivered with what resources. You expect them to agree, to be excited by the stronger future results, if they see the purpose clearly.*

In other "change" examples, you may need to:

O Pitch a contentious recommendation. To show an audience how your proposal is exactly what they need, when looked at in a new light.

O Persuade leadership to support a major change in strategy e.g. an organisational redesign. To convince an audience that the new plan may be a fundamental shift, but one that is required.

O Convince a team that a new vision is desirable and achievable. To acknowledge the old way got us this far, but now, today, we choose to head in a new direction.

Belonging **Scenarios:**

We all want to belong to a community, a tribe, a family. Your audience are people, and people want to feel a connection of trust with others. Sometimes these feelings of belonging and trust are more important than anything else.

For example: *Mohammed is making a presentation to a potential new client. They know the service that he provides. They tell Mohammed that they certainly need the service. They seem uncertain if they want to invest in building a collaborative working relationship with Mohammed. Mohammed feels this is a situation where he wants to build a connection and trust with them.*

In other "belonging" examples, you may need to:

O Make a vital partner team feel appreciated and valued. So they know how much you admire what they bring to the table, encouraging them to continue working hard on your priorities.

O Acknowledge that we have come through a tough time. Before we can understand where we are and choose where to go next, we need to soothe tensions, give people an opportunity to discuss, a moment to reflect on their thoughts and those of others.

O Encourage the team to collaborate and work well together. Visions and plans can wait, for now we want to develop team spirit and resilience.

Actions **Scenarios:**

Getting things done takes clarity, focus, and hard graft. An audience rarely wants to be "ordered around", but that does not mean they don't want to be directed. As long as you are well placed to do so, they will appreciate you making the important decisions, clearly articulating instructions, and tracking progress.

For example: *Ali is telling the team about the upgraded system for raising and processing invoices. They do not care about the details. They have no authority over choices made. They do not need to love what Ali is telling them to do. Ali needs them to complete four steps: launch the new application on their computer, complete their registration, take the one-hour training, and send confirmation of the first three back to him.*

In other "actions" examples, you may need to:

O Set priority expectations. Lay out goals for us collectively and individually to achieve.

O Direct on the next steps needed to move the project forward. Explain what needs to be done, in what way, and by whom.

O Instruct on the team/company processes. Teach how things are done correctly (so they are not done incorrectly) and consistently within present systems.

SELECT

In Summary

Step 2:
SELECT Your Prez-type:

You consider the direction arrow you set as your **prez-intent** and select a nearby **prez-type**.

You may pick the prez-type nearest to your arrow, or one nearby based on other important factors.

These factors may include:

- O the prez-type you find easiest.
- O how your audience sees you.
- O the form of your content.

hero

magician

explorer

maverick

jester

sage

lover

student

everyman

creator

ruler

caregiver

Step 2: SELECT Your Prez-type

What Next?

You have **set a prez-intent**. You feel more confident in what you are trying to achieve. What now? How does this help?

It helps you make a stronger next decision: **the type of presentation to design and deliver.**

I don't wear the same clothes to every occasion; sometimes I don a dinner jacket, sometimes I throw on a sweatshirt, sometimes I put on a business suit, occasionally I get into gym gear. In each case I choose the type of clothing for the occasion. Sometimes the choice is easy (my one dinner jacket and bow-tie); sometimes the choice is tricky (which shirt to wear to a first date?).

You don't deliver a presentation in the same way every time. **You select the type of presentation (prez-type) based on the situation (prez-intent).**

Your second step is to **SELECT your prez-type.**

At times the choice is easy and at others, it requires some extra thought.

Yes, But How?

In the next few pages, we will **introduce you to twelve prez-types.** Each prez-type guides you to a different way of presenting.

Each prez-type encourages your audience to respond in a particular way.

Your prez-intent focusses these twelve down to a small number of prez-types to select from. We will describe how to select the best one for you and your specific presentation.

Where Do the Twelve Prez-types Come From?

Our twelve **prez-types** are inspired by the archetypes proposed by Carl Jung.[12] Ours are: **sage, explorer, hero, magician, maverick, jester, lover, everyman, caregiver, ruler, creator** and **student**.

If you have come across the archetypes, you will recognise some of these. You may have seen them in personality profiling (e.g. MBTI[13]), marketing theory,[14] acting classes,[15] screenwriting,[16] or countless other endeavours that connect back to Jung's work.

It is more likely that you have never spent any time considering archetypes. Don't worry. They make intuitive sense very quickly.

They offer an ideal map of twelve distinct and differentiated types of communication style.

Let's briefly introduce each one.

Introducing...

...Twelve Prez-types

Hero

As your **hero** prez-type you convey a compelling cause and inspire commitment.

Magician

As your **magician** prez-type you attest that the impossible is now possible.

Explorer

As your **explorer** prez-type you drive curiosity and chart discovery.

Maverick

As your **maverick** prez-type you provoke dissatisfaction in the status quo.

Sage

As your **sage** prez-type you evaluate and then express expertise.

Jester

As your **jester** prez-type you connect people together by bringing the fun!

Student

As your **student** prez-type you digest the information to teach the layperson.

Lover

As your **lover** prez-type you make people feel valued and valuable.

Creator

As your **creator** prez-type you eagerly demonstrate the usefulness of your creation.

Everyman

As your **everyman** prez-type you unify behind a common purpose and a collective responsibility.

Ruler

As your **ruler** prez-type you establish direction and direct action.

Caregiver

As your **caregiver** prez-type you guide progress and provide guardrails.

How Do I Choose Between Twelve?

Each prez-type has a position around the prez-intent compass.

For example:

magician prez-type sits just to the right of change.

jester prez-type sits just above **belonging**.

creator prez-type sits equally between actions and knowledge.

In setting your **prez-intent you have drawn an arrow pointing towards one or two prez-types – but you can consider any prez-type nearby.**

E.g. you may have set a **prez-intent** of change.

Your arrow points directly north. This gives you up to four prez-types to consider: **explorer, hero, magician,** and **maverick.**

You select one of these prez-types.

How Will This Help?

Each **prez-type** enables you to present in a style that encourages your audience to listen and respond in the way that you want. This is a powerful insight from Carl Jung's work. He wrote of a "collective unconscious" – how all of us, regardless of culture and background, have consistent ways we respond to our experiences of the world. To put it into our working lives, there are universally recognisable types of presenter, where each will consistently evoke distinct types of response from your audience.

If you create and deliver a **ruler-type** presentation, you will talk with assuredness, clarity, and authority. This will inspire your audience to listen attentively to your instructions (and be clear on actions to take).

If you create and deliver a **jester-type** presentation, you will speak with playfulness, jollity, and irreverence. This will inspire your audience to stay relaxed and enjoy their time with you (and build a sense of **belonging** with you and each other).

If you are keen to learn more about this now, go to the end of "Part 4: GOING FURTHER – A Little More On Archetypes". Otherwise, we ask you to trust us when we say **The Prez Method** works, and to join us moving forward.

You select a **prez-type** near to where you marked your **prez-intent** because this **prez-type** will foster the audience response that you are looking for. Your **prez-type** supports your **prez-intent**.

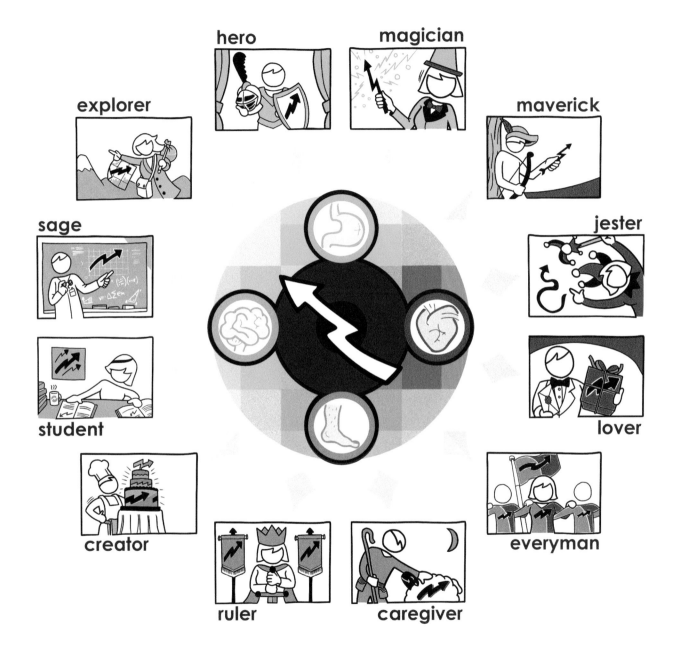

For example, you have set your prez-intent as knowledge. Perhaps you need to take everyone through the insights from a recent market research report.

You look at your pointer and find four options:

O **explorer:** the audience learns new knowledge through each discovery.

O **sage:** the audience accesses vital knowledge through your experience.

O **student:** the audience understands knowledge through your summaries.

O **creator:** the audience is given the knowledge necessary to use the thing you have created.

Any of these four **prez-types** are viable options to select.

The **prez-types** closest to your **prez-intent** mark are the most likely to evoke the response that you want. In this instance, **sage prez-type** and **student prez-type** are perfectly placed to help people learn knowledge.

However, there are many reasons why you might instead consider **explorer prez-type** and **creator prez-type** as alternatives.

What are these factors? What should be part of your consideration as you decide? How do you decide?

How to Decide Which to Select?

There can be many things to consider. Here are three that come up regularly:

Your Preference

There will be some prez-types that you feel most comfortable using. If you love being the explorer prez-type, that is a great reason to select it.

If you find the thought of using a sage prez-type unnerving, choose an adjacent prez-type. Here that would be explorer or student.

Your Audience

Your role or history with this audience may mean you have an "equity" that you want to maintain for consistency. Say you are the expert in this topic; it will feel obvious to select the sage prez-type.

Or you may want to shock your audience out of inertia, so you select a prez-type different to what they expect. Maybe you surprise them by being an explorer prez-type.

Your Content

The topic itself may fit well with one of the prez-types. The very nature of the information you want to share lends itself to a particular choice.

If you are introducing your audience to a new process for how the company does initiative launches, it could be that creator prez-type is a sound selection.

One of these factors may trump all others or a mixture may feel important. You consider your options and select a prez-type.

It is okay to pick the **prez-type** nearest to your **prez-intent** mark. This makes the decision feel easy. You are capable of embodying any of these twelve **prez-types.** Be brave and pick the closest.

OR

It is okay to move a step or two away to select a **prez-type** which feels best for this presentation. Your preference, your audience, or the content itself may persuade you to adjust to find the best fit.

Sometimes it will feel obvious which **prez-type** to select. Sometimes it will feel tricky. Whichever it is, take a deep breath and make a choice.

Can I Select More Than One Prez-type?

Yes, you can, and there are scenarios where this is what we recommend. But it adds complexity, so we will look at this later. For now, we will keep things simple-ish, and guide you to only select one prez-type.

Here are some micro-examples to give you a clearer picture of how this can work in practice.

e.g.1 Sofia must convince the team that a new organisation structure will help fix the business. She wants them to feel good about it too.

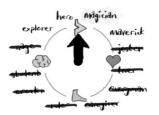

Sofia sees her prez-intent arrow pointing at **magician prez-type.** This works for her.

She selects **magician prez-type** and moves onto step 3.

e.g.2 Ethan needs to brief his team on new legislation and its impact on the business processes. This falls within his role remit, but he is not an expert in this area.

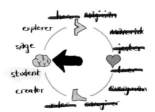

Ethan sees he has **four prez-types** to choose from: **explorer, sage, student,** and **creator.** He considers the nearest two: **sage** and **student.**

He does not feel like an expert in the topic (although, loves being the true expert in other areas). He feels much more comfortable keeping things simple for himself and straightforward for the audiences.

He selects the **student prez-type** and moves on to step 3.

e.g.3 Fatima is planning a presentation at an industry conference. She wants everyone to see her and her company as being trustworthy and credible, at the centre of the best work being done. She wants people in the audience to go to her company's website to learn more about what they offer.

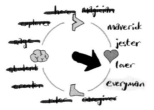

Fatima reviews her **four primary prez-type** options: **jester, lover, everyman,** and maybe **maverick.**

She dismisses **maverick** and **jester prez-types** as being unhelpful in establishing credibility. Fatima considers **lover prez-type** as she feels it would encourage trust and help her to talk passionately about the fabulous work being done by so many companies represented by the audience. However, she selects a prez-type that will help get the action she wants: people to go to her company's website.

She selects the **everyman prez-type** and moves on to step 3.

Moving from **Strategy to Execution**

We have covered the first two steps of **The Prez Method**. Two choices have been made: Set + Select. They may have been easy choices or tortuously difficult selections. Either way it is worth pausing for a moment to acknowledge you are now moving from strategy to execution.

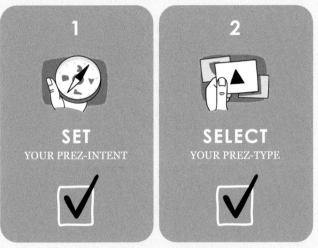

1	2	3	4
SET YOUR PREZ-INTENT ✓	**SELECT** YOUR PREZ-TYPE ✓	**SHARPEN** YOUR PREZ-CONTENT ☐	**SHIFT** YOUR PREZ-STYLE ☐
Two strategic choices made: the audience response that you are aiming for and the prez-type you will use.		Next, we explore how your choice of prez-type will help you improve the messaging, content, and structure of your presentation.	Afterwards, we explain how the choice of prez-type will also transform your presentation style.

It is possible that these two steps are enough for you. You have a clear sense of what you want to achieve (**prez-intent**) and a creative seed to spark from (**prez-type**). Combined with your experience and bravery, this might be enough to work out for yourself how this will influence how you design and deliver your presentation.

If you are like us, you will appreciate more help and guidance. We continue on to Step 3: Sharpen your **prez-content**. We will explain how your **prez-type** helps you make vital decisions regarding your presentation: your message, your content choices, and your presentation structure.

SHARPEN

In Summary

Step 3:

SHARPEN Your Prez-content:

It is hard to be creatively brilliant with nothing but a blank piece of paper and a mountain of content to organise.

The prez-type you selected gives you a guiding hand on how to sharpen all parts of your presentation.

The prez-type assists you to:

1) **Hone your messaging:** phrase the meaning considering your prez-type.

2) **Shave your info:** prioritise and deprioritise content considering your prez-type.

3) **Chart your structure:** sequence your content considering your prez-type.

These can be a final trim just before the presentation or they can be a slow and meticulous sculpting of the whole thing.

Step 3: **SHARPEN** Your Prez-content

The Joy of Pencil Sharpening

In our house, we love using a quality pencil sharpener. There is a simple pleasure in taking a stack of pencils and meticulously shaving each one to a fine point.

The joy returns each time we write or draw with a perfectly sharpened pencil (for us normally to battle codeword and sudoku puzzles).

Can we find similar delight in sharpening the message, content, and structure of our presentation?

Presentation Sharpening

You probably have a good sense of the many things you could talk about in your presentation. How do you craft and refine this into your words and visuals? It can feel like you are drawing with a blunt pencil. Each way we try to flow through our content makes our presentation feel rough and ill-formed.

We need to get out our sharpener and start shaving.

We consider three key questions:

1) How to hone your messaging (phrase your meaning)?
2) How to shave your info (prioritise and deprioritise)?
3) How to chart your structure (sequence)?

You use the **prez-type** to guide your answers to these questions, leading to a more precise form of your **prez-content**.

When you are a confident "Prez Method superhero", this can be intuitive. For example:

> Melanie is a maverick master and selects the **maverick prez-type** for her next presentation. Her first draft for her main message is *"I recommend we invest in getting back our lapsed buyers."* She has a think for a few minutes, letting her maverick-self drive her thinking. She effortlessly types out, *"Buyers: ignore the new, court the lapsed."*

Most of us are not like Melanie, a master of each prez-type (although we will be in time). We want a guiding hand...

SHARPEN
YOUR PREZ-CONTENT

Hone Your Messaging	Shave Your Info	Chart Your Structure
You have a main message to share, with additional points to put across.	However much information you have, you need to trim some of it!	You map out the arrangement and sequence of your content.
You precisely shape your messaging so the deeper meaning is manifest.	You whittle your content down to the most pertinent and interesting.	You define the through line, from your first idea to your last.

Phrase as your prez-type	Prioritise as your prez-type	Sequence as your prez-type
Consider the message: *"The office shuts early today so decorators can paint meeting rooms."*	When you place yourself into the shoes of a specific prez-type you find it easier to know what to prioritise and what to deprioritise.	Each prez-type gives you a hint for how to open and how to close your presentation.
E.g. Bring to mind a typical **ruler**. How would they word this? It would be a directive like *"Decorators are refreshing our main meeting room tonight. I expect you all out of the office by 3 p.m. I will lock the doors at 3:05."*	E.g. The **hero prez-type** is going to prioritise content that emphasises the vital nature of the goal. They will deprioritise anything that celebrates their own achievements.	Each prez-type encourages you to arrange your content into various modes of structure.
E.g. Bring to mind a typical **jester**. How would they phrase their message? It would be a witticism like *"Decorators are in to paint the office blue. So we are off to paint the town red."*	E.g. The **lover prez-type** is going to prioritise content that praises and celebrates the audience. They will deprioritise anything unflattering.	E.g. The **maverick prez-type** is more likely to choose a two-structure comparing the old (wrong) way with a new (right) way.
		E.g. The **sage prez-type** is more likely to choose a logic structure, setting up a hypothesis and stepping methodically towards a proof.

Trimming a Few Edges or a Brutal Carving?

How far should you go to **sharpen your prez-content**? The choice is entirely yours.

It will depend on factors like how much time you have and how important the presentation is. It may be a final trim or it may be a carving from scratch.

A final trim:

You may have a presentation that is largely complete. You use the **prez-type** to guide your hand as you refine the messaging and judiciously shave off elements of the content. You make a quick map of the flow through your ideas.

A carving from scratch:

You may be days, or even weeks, away from the presentation itself. You use your **prez-type** selection as the design brief for all parts of your presentation. Almost every part of the design of the presentation is influenced by the prez-type.

Below is a short example of the latter – where the **prez-type** inspires all aspects of the crafting of the presentation.

Ava has an important internal presentation coming up. She is leading a project for her company, toymaker company "GeloBricks", to understand how new packaging options might be used for their toys. She is working with EcoPacket, an innovator in ecological packaging. Their newest line, "Clixboard", could help meet their green targets while still protecting the product through the supply chain.

Ava is bringing together a multifunctional group of leaders from across the business. Her aim is to introduce Clixboard to them. Ava wants all functions to see Clixboard as a positive option going forward, and to think about implications from their functional perspective e.g. Marketing thinking through its value in future advertising.

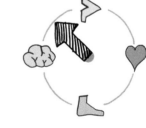

SET: Ava has set her **prez-intent** as **knowledge + change**.

SELECT: Ava has selected the **explorer prez-type**.

Ava goes to the chapter on **explorer prez-type**, reads it to get ideas, and crafts her presentation.

Hone Your Messaging

Ava's starting message is:

"Clixboard is the priority packaging technology for our future packaging and supply chain initiatives."

This is almost sending her to sleep. She knows this needs work!

Ava fashions the message into a **revelation**. She sketches a few different phrases and lands finally with:

"We may have found our transformative packaging solution: let me introduce you to Clixboard."

Ava feels this better gives the right tone for the presentation.

Shave Your Info

EcoPacket have shared with Ava an overabundance of information: tech specs, use cases, case studies, costs, usage tests, and more.

Ava pauses and thinks like an **explorer**. She will prioritise content that helps them see Clixboard as she does – to experience its key benefits. She can get into more mundane details at a later meeting; for now she will cover a lot of ground at speed. She wants to highlight major points of interest – things that are new. Ava works through her content pulling out the most important and most interesting highlights.

Ava has many initial thoughts on how it could be brought into the supply chain, and how it could be used as a core element within the marketing messaging. Again, she considers her persona as an **explorer** and admits to herself that she needs to leave the audience free to come across the important conclusions themselves. So she replaces content summarising her perspectives with time to discuss and consider the audience's observations.

Ava is left with an extensive set of content, but with a clear sense of what is most important to include and what can be left on the cutting room floor.

Chart Your Structure

Ava reads the advice in the **explorer prez-type** chapter. It gives her some starting ideas on structures.

Ava decides to use an "Epic Journey" structure for the central part of her presentation. She organises her information as follows:

1) **Pack the Rucksack**: crucial information and terminology that will be key to recognising important facts later in the journey e.g. reminder of green targets; base specification needs for packaging.

2) **First Fresh Discoveries**: an initial look at the features and benefits of Clixboard. Example packaging brought for the team to explore. Time for observations from the audience.

3) **Fun Side Paths**: a brief overview of the limitations of Clixboard, including increased costs, specific product lines where Clixboard is not yet appropriate.

4) **Major Discoveries**: prototype of a key product line with Clixboard packaging. Time to show how it solves a key wish – more prominent on-shelf presence.

5) **Reflecting at the Summit**: reinforce key benefits (and a few limitations). A brief overview of the work to come to get into real practicalities.

6) **Unpacking at Home**: summary of everything that we have found. Aligning on next steps.

Ava feels great about the flow for the presentation. She feels confident it is doing what she needs it to do.

Moving On...

Until now your role has to been to craft your presentation. To sit at your desk taking time to consider choices, experiment with different options, to write and draw and lay out your presentation.

It is time to change your role. Now you will become the person speaking the presentation: delivering your words in real time. How will you shift your delivery style into a presentation performance befitting the **prez-type**?

SHIFT

In Summary

Step 4:
SHIFT Your Prez-style:

You turn the **prez-type** that you selected into a spirit on your shoulder that whispers a single word or short mantra.

This inspires all parts of your delivery: your spoken and body language, your staging, and your use of visual aids.

explorer prez-type

"I am an explorer"

The **prez-type** provides you with a way to shift vital elements of your delivery. The result is your **prez-style**.

The amount you shift is up to you. This must still be an authentic version of you. It can be a small or major shift.

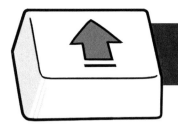

Step 4: **SHIFT Your Prez-style**

Look Closely at the Shift Key

The shift key on a keyboard is a magical thing. We use it every day without a thought for the truly extraordinary thing it does. By pressing it down while tapping on a letter key, it keeps the meaning the same and yet communicates something different. Sometimes the change is mechanical, sometimes subtle, sometimes transformative.

At its core "b" is the same as "B", and yet we have learnt that they can infer different things.

"Are YOU able to do this?" tells us something subtly different to *"Are you ABLE to do this?"*, which tells you something different to *"Are you able to do THIS?"* The same information but the shift key guides us, the reader, to interpret the meaning in different ways.

All this with only a single button on the keyboard. Add in **bold**, <u>underline</u>, *italics*, in ***combinations***, and we have only just begun. We have font size, font type, and font colour.

It is EASY to <u>**create**</u> a complete MₑsS of shifTIng **shapes**.

itistemptingtoleaveeverythingconsistentanddullandjustasconfusing.

We should marvel at the shift key. We should learn to harness its magical powers.

Everything is Sharpened, and Yet...

"Step 3: SHARPEN your prez-content" is complete. Your points are precise, your information is trimmed down to just the most vital, and you have a through line mapped out. Why do you need a Step 4: SHIFT your prez-style?

Because you are likely to "**regress to routine**". While you craft your presentation, you can make many decisions on how you intend to present your information. Yet, the moment you stand up to speak, as the social realities clarify in your mind, your adrenaline rises and you dive towards safety. You leap to your routine presentation style, your familiar and comfortable way of presenting.

How do you trigger a shift? How do you ensure your words, gestures, and movements match the prez-type that you selected?

Just Press "Shift"

With practice, you spontaneously switch into your selected **prez-type** just by deciding to do so.

*"Right! It is time for me to be my **hero prez-type**."*

This shifts you into your **prez-style**: your selected prez-type delivered in a way that is true to you.

We each have an inbuilt sense of what it means to be "heroic". If I tell a class of school children to walk around the room in a heroic way, they just can. They stride around confidently, with their chests puffed out, with an easy movement and yet with a readiness for action.

As adults, we may not feel the freedom of childhood, but we still have the ability to shift how we walk, gesture, and speak. In addition, we have the benefit of experience. Even the most timid amongst us has been brave at points in our lives. We have all had to gather up our courage to do something scary because we knew it was the right thing to do. This is being heroic.

If you tell yourself, *"Right! It is time for me to be my **hero prez-type**"*, you instinctively shift. You roll up your sleeves. You position yourself confidently in centre stage. You stand tall. You emphasise the vital importance of what we must try to achieve. You increase the vigour of your speaking tone. You add fervour to your gestures. You behave more heroically.

Each of the twelve prez-types are ways of speaking and moving that you have inside of you. Each is accessible to you. Some will be easier and some will take a little time to practise, but all twelve prez-types are at your disposal.

"Surrender" to Type

Once the presentation starts, you have so many things to be thinking about. You do not have the cognitive capacity to make a long analysis of how you will adapt every movement and gesture; how you will affect the articulation and tone of every syllable.

The time for intellectualisation is over. It is time to give your instinctive self a simple instruction and to trust it to act accordingly. You want one intuitive idea, accessible through one word. For example: "**hero**".

Actors talk of surrendering to their character's "actions and transactions"[17] – having a consistent origin for their reactions on stage. You do the same – **submit to the prez-type** and your delivery is imbued with the tone and feel that you want: your **prez-style**.

Authentically Me?

Each will be you. This is about adapting your authentic self. This is not about adding a mask or a false front. Your style of being the magician prez-type will be different to how someone else embodies it because it is your magician style.

The prez-type is universal; your prez-style is unique to you.

If you feel yourself stepping towards artifice, pause and reconnect with what **your version of this prez-type is**. Trust yourself.

Once you learn to shift into a prez-type, you approach your next challenge: how to maintain it?

Nothing Lasts Forever

This magical imbuement to talk and move as your **prez-style** will dissolve. Without focus and conscious attention you will **regress to routine**. The word that inspired you at the start will fade from memory and you will return to your standard way of presenting.

To counter this, you intermittently whisper your **prez-type** to yourself: *"be the hero"*. This clicks you back into the style that you want to embody.

If ever you feel yourself meandering back to your normal presenter type, let your **prez-type mantra** jolt you back into the style that you want.

You will learn how often you need to give yourself a reminder. Mentally you place your little finger over the shift key, ready to press whenever you lose the prez-style inside you.

Learn To Touch-type

Learning to touch-type takes a little practice, but the time it saves you can be hugely valuable. At first, you feel your fingers are sausages blindly bashing at the keyboard. Soon your hands are intuitively skipping across the keyboard at breakneck speed.

It also takes a little conscious practice to learn to shift into a prez-type. It is a habit, and habits need multiple repetitions.

Start safely and start slowly. Find low-risk scenarios where you can try out different prez-types. A few repetitions and your confidence will fly.

How Far to Go?

How far should you take your shift? Should it be a minor 5% shift, a noticeable 50% shift, or a transformative 100% shift?

If you have selected to be your explorer prez-type, how fully do you let this affect your persona?

You could make only a minor shift. You take on the role of a "scout". You use the language of travel: where we have been, where we are now, and where we are going. Perhaps you walk around the space a little more than you normally would?

You could make a noticeable shift. You become an "adventurer". You move with vigour and enthusiasm. You pause to highlight new and interesting elements, but otherwise you stay keen to keep exploring.

You could make a major shift. You become a true "trailblazer". You talk poetically about breaking boundaries and forging new paths, of magnificent vistas and energising progress. You maraud around the space, through the audience, and back again.

Any of these are valid choices. You choose! How far you take your version of the prez-type depends on your personality, the situation, and the content. You decide how big or small to make it.

When you make the shift small, your audience will only subconsciously perceive the transition. When you make the shift large, your audience will consciously notice the transformation. Either is valid.

How This Might Look

Using the **prez-types** as a shift key for your mind, voice, and body has an empowering effect. It transforms you from your learnt "routine style" to one of twelve authentic versions of you. Soon you will be making delivery choices like these:

creator prez-type

"I am a creator"

magician prez-type

"I am a magician"

lover prez-type

"I am a lover"

This may be enough info for you on SHIFT. If you want to get on with learning about the twelve prez-types in detail, move on to Part 3: DO IT. If you are keen to learn more about how to transform your delivery, keep reading!

The Versatile Presenter

Typesetting

Typography is full of fascinating terms:[18] serif, ascender, aperture, kerning, ligature, leading, etc. Each refers to something that will intrinsically alter the form and style of the written text.

As you prepare and practise your presentation delivery, you have four primary things to consider. They lack the mystery of the typographic terms, but they are just as important to you.

SHIFT
YOUR PREZ-STYLE

Spoken Language

Each prez-type has a form of language.

The **magician** uses simple and yet mysterious phrases.

The **hero** uses emotive words to articulate the quest, but simple action words to describe the progress.

The **everyman** talks of "we". The **lover** talks of "you". The **creator** talks of "it".

Don't let the style words that you use be an accident.

Body Language

Each prez-type has a shape to its gestures.

The **ruler** stands planted, facing squarely out towards their audience. Gestures are clean and clear.

The **maverick** leans nonchalantly on one hip, gesturing dismissively.

Knowing what to do with our arm movements can feel stifling. Don't overthink it, let your prez-type inspire the movements that you make.

Staging

Each prez-type utilises the space differently.

The **creator** places their content (creation) centre stage. They beckon the audience to come closer.

The **explorer** travels around the space, pausing to marvel at their discoveries.

The **jester** bounces around the stage, eagerly calling on volunteers to join in.

Your prez-type affects how you lay out and move around your space.

Visual Aids

Each prez-type prefers specific types of visuals.

The **sage** walks you through chart after chart on the monitor, then steps away to just talk directly.

The **student** shares a few slides before going to a flipchart to draw out their simplified picture of what is happening.

The **caregiver** puts up a poster with the guidelines to follow.

Let your prez-type lead how you visualise your main content.

Case Study: "One Scenario; Four Shifts"

Let's now look at a fictional case study. Here is the background.

Liam is the team leader for a marketing operations team. A recent financial audit of all invoicing processes has brought up some significant concerns. Their score came out as "unsatisfactory" (three out of five). Liam was informed that four out of five was the minimum expectation. If they score the same at the next audit, there will be some serious implications: penalties and perhaps jobs lost.

Liam has experience of similar challenges: he knows he needs an expert in the team to ensure financial proceedures are being followed. Liam has gone to the regional leader to get agreement and secure funding for a new headcount on the team.

Liam has hired Jane. Jane has twenty-five years of experience in managing and leading invoicing processes. Jane has worked with marketing operations people in the past. She is the perfect fit.

Jane has enthusiastically agreed to join the team as the new finance leader.

Liam and Jane have met to decide on a plan. Each member of the team will meet with Jane, then align on individual priorities, then meet with Liam within one week to update on progress.

Liam will make a short presentation to the team to allay any fears, introduce Jane and her role, and summarise the plan.

We imagine four parallel universes. In each, the context is different in some important ways that encourage Liam to make distinct choices.

In each, **Liam sets a different prez-intent** based on how he reads the situation and the needs of his audience. In each, **Liam selects a different prez-type**.

You will see how these four presentations will feel very different to the audience based on the strategic choices that Liam has made. The way the audience responds to Liam will vary by the ways he has flexed his presentation style.

Story 1: Liam as Student

Liam believes the priority is to educate the team in what happened and how the plan will work. Liam sets his **prez-intent** = knowledge.

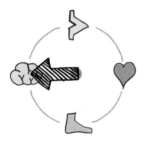

He considers his options, and quickly selects **student** as his **prez-type**.

He has had to learn so much so quickly about this – he can help fast track the team's understanding too.

He has sharpened the content, concentrating on sharing a digestible summary of key information.

Liam sets the room out with chairs in two semi-circular rows. He places two seats at the front and sits in the first.

He starts his presentation with his message, a learning: *"I have learned that we have an issue we cannot fix alone."*

He works through a simplified explanation of the issue at hand. He shares a few data charts, clarifying things of importance and skipping past details. He emphasises that he is no expert, but talking to the auditors it is clear that we need to raise our score. He steps across to the flipchart and writes:
"3/5 = bad; 4/5 = good; 5/5 = great."

Throughout, Liam keeps his language simple. He explains any technical terms. He focusses on being curious in learning more about the audit process and how we fix it. He is full of admiration for the expertise that Jane will bring.

Liam invites Jane forward. He explains, *"Jane has the exact experience that we need. Twenty-five years of working on similar invoicing systems, including working with marketing operations teams like ours."*

Liam summarises a longer conversation that he had with Jane. *"What helped me most was when Jane pulled things together into a metaphor. A Formula 1 car needs to regularly come into the pits to change tyres – we, the team, are the drivers of the business, but if we don't occasionally come in to let Jane check that all the tyres still have strong grip, we will soon be spinning off the track. We need to regularly connect with Jane to make sure all our invoicing documentation is as it should be."*

Liam stays attentive to his audience, regularly checking if anything is unclear or not yet understood.

Liam briefly explains the plan: meet Jane, align plan, update Liam.

He closes emphasising his main message: *"We cannot fix this alone. We need Jane's guidance."*

Story 2: Liam as Hero

Liam believes the priority is to inspire the team to see this as the #1 priority. Liam sets his **prez-intent** = change.

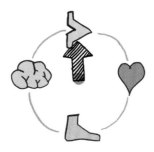

He considers his options, and quickly selects **hero** as his **prez-type**.

There is nothing new or exciting about what needs to be done. But, if they don't act, the sanctions will be severe. They must act to protect the work that they do.

He has sharpened the content, cutting much of the explanation so he can focus on what is at stake.

Liam sets the room out with chairs in rows. He makes sure the lights are down a little, but there is a strong light centre stage where he will stand. There is no monitor for slides, just a single flipchart with the phrase *"To protect the work we do..."*

He starts his presentation with his message, a mission: *"To protect the work we do we need to buckle down and fix our invoicing issues."*

He tells the story of what will happen at the next audit if nothing changes. He lists the issues the auditors will find, he describes the moment when the team receives its second score of three out of five, and he paints a distressing picture of the likely implications: penalties, disruption to our work, and friends lost from the team.

He pauses to let this sink in. Then says, *"We must not let this happen."*

He shifts his energy to the challenges ahead. He omits details; these will come later.

He sets out the crux of the matter: *"Who can lead our work?"*, and introduces Jane. *"We need the guiding hand of a true expert. As you know, headcount has been locked for this year. However, I went to Mary, our VP, and sold her on our need for her support to get this fixed. She has agreed to fund the headcount to bring Jane into the team. We must respect the trust that Mary is putting in us all."*

Throughout, Liam talks with vigour and conviction. He literally rolls up his sleeves, and moves around confidently. He talks impassionedly about the importance of what we do. Nothing is sugar-coated: this will be uninteresting work.

Liam briefly explains the plan: meet Jane, align plan, update Liam.

He closes emphasising his main message: *"To protect the work we do, we must fix these issues."*

Story 3: Liam as Lover

Liam can feel the tension across the team. Nothing will happen unless he can get everyone to relax and trust each other (and Jane). Liam sets his **prez-intent** = **belonging**.

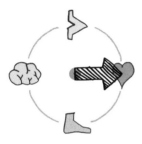

He considers his options, and quickly selects **lover** as his **prez-type**.

Each member of the team will be worried about their own jobs. He wants everyone to feel appreciated.

He has sharpened the content, throwing out anything overly negative, and bringing in elements eulogising about the great work of the team.

Liam invites everyone into the main meeting room. Chairs are set out in a relaxed atmosphere. There are pastries and other nice snacks in reach of everyone. He has ordered in nice coffee (and other drinks) for people to enjoy. Everyone has had a chance to grab food and a drink, so Liam stands up to deliver his short speech.

He starts with a praising message to everyone present: *"No one solves challenges like this team."* He segues into three stories of recent challenges that this great team has come across, and the brilliant ways that they solved them. He calls out a range of people by name, but ensures the greatest praise is reserved for the team as a whole.

Liam connects this team's brilliant problem-solving skills with the great business results that they are hitting. Liam reminds them of recent awards won by the team.

Liam smiles broadly. He talks with fulsome admiration for everyone present. This is not just a good team; this is the best team.

He talks about the problem. *"You have this! I have just given you three recent examples of harder problems that you have solved. However, I want to make this as easy as I can for you. I am bringing to you a new finance leader, Jane. If you want personal training on the updated invoice approval software, she is here. If you want definition checks, she is here. If you want a second opinion on your invoice priorities, she is here."*

Liam runs a brief discussion session to hear ideas from the group on how they want to go about fixing the invoicing issue.

Liam offers the three-step plan as a potential process, but highlights that they can each deliver this as they see fit. He has booked time in each person's diary for next week in case they have questions or anything they want to talk about.

Liam closes with his main message. *"You are the greatest – you've got this."*

Story 4: Liam as Ruler

Liam can see that it all comes down to execution. The team needs to complete a series of vital steps. Liam sets his **prez-intent** = actions.

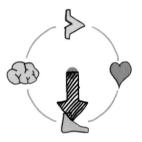

He considers his options, and quickly selects **ruler** as his **prez-type**.

This will be dull work. He will need to set definitive expectations and show that he will be closely tracking progress. Only then will this issue be solved efficiently.

He has sharpened the content, minimising details on what has happened and why it is important. He will mostly talk about the targets he is setting, the authority he is handing on to Jane to oversee plans, and how he will expect regular progress updates.

Liam calls everyone into the meeting room. The chairs are set out in rigid rows. He has created a good-sized stage space at the front with a large screen projecting his message, a directive: *"Fixing Invoice Process is Everyone's #1 Priority."*

Liam walks to stand in the centre of the stage and pauses, waiting for total quiet and full focus. He talks firmly throughout. He gives everyone eye contact. His sentences are short and clear. He rarely moves from centre stage.

Liam explains the seriousness of the recent poor audit score. *"This result is unacceptable."* He states that fixing this issue is now *"my number one priority, which means it is your number one priority."*

He briefly explains the data from the recent audit. He acknowledges the team is bringing in strong business results. *"These invoice process issues will not be allowed to derail ongoing strong results."*

Liam introduces Jane, highlighting how he is passing on significant authority to her. *"When Jane tells you to complete a step, I want you all to consider it a priority direction from me."*

Liam then takes everyone slowly through the process: 1) go to Jane today to book a first meeting with her; 2) meet with Jane where you will lead a review of status on all invoices (and answer her questions); 3) meet with me next week to summarise your progress.

Liam checks they understand. *"Anything unclear? My door is always open on this. If you see any barrier to progress, I expect you to tell me on the same day."*

Liam closes on his main message, *"Fixing this is everyone's number one priority."*

Closing Part 2: **THE PREZ METHOD**

We have walked carefully through all four steps. **SET, SELECT, SHARPEN,** and **SHIFT**.

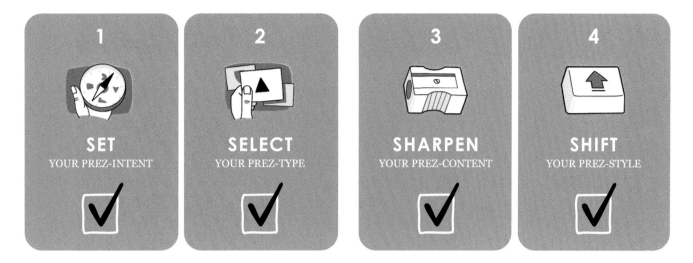

It is time to move from learning about **The Prez Method** to start exploring specific prez-types.

Part 3: DO IT is where we dive into the deep end for each prez-type. Each chapter offers you a treasure trove of tips and techniques. We suggest you jump in to see what you can find.

Perhaps, bring to mind a real presentation coming up, select the prez-type you want to embody, and go to the associated chapter. Or simply go to the prez-type that intrigues you most.

I Want to Learn More First

If you do not feel ready to explore Part 3: DO IT, you have another option. If you are itching to learn more about **The Prez Method**, you can jump to Part 4: GOING FURTHER. Here you will find more on:

- ○ Top tips on how to get the most out of each step of **The Prez Method**.
- ○ Guidance for presentations where you want to combine more than one prez-type.
- ○ Perspectives on how to make sure you stay as the authentic version of you, whichever prez-type you select.

3

» DO IT »

hero

magician

explorer

maverick

sage

jester

student

lover

creator

everyman

ruler

caregiver

Part 3: **DO IT**

The next twelve chapters help you put **The Prez Method** into practice. There is a twelve-page chapter for each of the twelve prez-types. Each chapter is packed full of tips and idea starters for that prez-type.

We start with the **sage prez-type** and work round clockwise until we get to the **student prez-type**.

For any presentation, once you have selected a likely **prez-type**, read through the associated chapter. This will ground you in the **prez-type** so you feel confident in your choice. It will then offer you tonnes of action ideas for how you may sharpen the presentation design and shift your delivery.

Each chapter is laid out in exactly the same way:

○ *First to third page:* An introduction to the prez-type. Includes examples from fiction and real life to give you an intuitive sense of the essence of the prez-type.

○ *Fourth to sixth page,* **When to Select**: Situations when this prez-type is an ideal choice. Tasks (intentional actions) to focus on. A spectrum of "intensity levels" of the prez-type to consider (from 🌶 mild to 🌶🌶🌶 hot!).

○ *Seventh to eighth page,* **Shape Sharpeners**: How to craft your message. How to prioritise your content. How you might structure your content.

○ *Ninth to eleventh page,* **Shift Keys**: How to guide your audience to listen in the way you intend. Tips on spoken and body language, staging and visual aids. How to manage your notes. Ways to interact with your audience and thoughts on how to ready yourself before the presentation.

○ *Twelfth page,* **Prez-type Watch-outs**: Prez-type pitfalls to avoid. And **Prez-type Pairings**: Other prez-types to combine with.

Go to *www.versatilepresenter.com/resources* to download a useful template to make notes as you read.

Sage

Explorer

Hero

Magician

Maverick

Jester

Lover

Everyman

Caregiver

Ruler

Creator

Student

Sage

Sage

curator

geek

expert

professor

academic

guru

doyen(ne)

As a **sage** prez-type you evaluate and then express expertise.

As a sage-type presenter you **educate** your audience. You **evaluate the available data,** analysis and insights. You explain facts and theories. You provide the **latest and best thinking** in your tight subject area.

You **educate your audience to the depth they desire:** complex reality or simplified formula, specific case study or abstract model. You answer their questions. You welcome intellectual debate. You willingly offer opinion.

The Essence of the Sage

> *"The more I learn,*
> *the more I realize how*
> *much I don't know."*
> Albert Einstein

From Fiction: Some sages educate the hero: Keating (Robin Williams) in *Dead Poets Society*, Yoda in *Star Wars*, or Mr Miyagi in *The Karate Kid*.

Other sages are focussed on solving essential problems themselves (rather than enabling some inferior thinker). Hermione Granger in the Harry Potter stories rolls-up her metaphorical sleeves to overcome knotty conundrums. Sherlock Holmes uses his encyclopaedic knowledge of criminology and pathology to solve an array of impenetrable mysteries.

Some sages appear onscreen only briefly to offer cryptic answers to priority questions, like Rafiki from *The Lion King*. Or they solve the thorniest puzzle, as astrophysicist, Rich Parnell, does in *The Martian*, as he rushes into NASA HQ to provide the manoeuvre that offers astronaut Mark Watney (Matt Damon) hope for an unlikely rescue from the surface of Mars.

From Real World: Confucius, Plato, and Aristotle not only thought great thoughts but found ways to teach them to the world. The Royal Institution in London has maintained a similar calling, staging lectures for over 200 years to connect "as many people as possible to the world of science". [19]

Modern examples abound. The nature documentaries of Sir David Attenborough. [20] TED Talk speakers with erudite minds sharing their best ideas (google Hans Rosling and Larry Lessig for some of our favourites). Pioneering stateswomen like Condoleezza Rice (former United States Secretary of State and National Security Advisor) now sharing her deep learning with students as director of the Hoover Institution at Stanford University.

Being your sage prez-type helps you **educate your audience** in what is certainly true, what is probably true, and what is possibly true. You are open and eager to share **fundamental theories**, discuss **alternative explanations**, introduce **new interpretations**, and provide **balanced assessments.**

 # Sage: **When to Select**

Choose to be a sage prez-type when you have evaluated an important topic you have expertise in. You want to expand the knowledge and understanding of your audience.

Select the sage prez-type when you want to...

...share a summary of analysis.	You have done an in-depth analysis of all the research on a topic. You are tasked to share the comprehensive summary of the key data and learnings with the team. You will also spotlight important details. You will do all you can to answer their questions.	*e.g. You are to present a full overview of key consumer and market insights. You summarise key data and the implications for the team's business.*
...share knowledge to inform a decision.	You have been asked to share specific knowledge with your audience, so that they can make better informed decisions. You have in-depth expertise that is not well understood by the Leadership Team, but is pertinent to a business decision to be made.	*e.g. You are the expert on the genetic modification of foods. You brief the brand leader on the science and implications so they can decide whether to include GM ingredients in the product.*
...scrutinise a subject in detail.	You have a class ready to learn. You have checked the knowledge they need and ascertained their present level of understanding. You are ready to educate them across a topic, test their understanding, and pass on your insights.	*e.g. You lecture a yearly class to new brand managers on vital aspects of marketing theory. They need to grasp the standard models and some of the latest ideas.*
...explain the uncertainty in a complex case.	You have a team making important decisions based on imperfect data and simplistic interpretations. You need them to comprehend the subtle differences between what is fact and what is conjecture, so they have a better reading of the probabilities and risks involved.	*e.g. You are presenting a full review of the uses of artificial intelligence in online marketing. You counter the myths, lay out the real success stories, and highlight potential risks.*

Sage **Task:** You are there to...

Check that you can focus on the right thing. The sage prez-type is best when you want to...

...evaluate »

You **evaluate** the facts and figures. You **evaluate** which theories best fit the situation. You **evaluate** all the relevant interpretations to come to the best one.

...educate »

You **educate** the audience in the facts and figures. You **educate** them on fascinating theories and interpretations. You **educate** them on the implications.

As you educate your audience and expand their thinking, you may consider one or more of the following:

scrutinise »

You analyse the available evidence. You identify the core facts, bring to light the root causes, and offer likely explanations. You take the time to define fundamental principles, subtle nuances and the underlying factors involved. You bring this together to précis your conclusions.

theorise »

You work through models, abstractions, axioms, and more. You convey wisdom and insight. You share models and methods to explain complex areas of knowledge. You test your audience's understanding, pulling them deeper and deeper into the fascinating topic.

deduce »

You assess the information and evidence available. You measure results, compare with key benchmarks, and determine the significance of each element. You calculate more potential explanations. You pass expert judgement based on pre-agreed criteria. You express your final expert appraisal.

lecture »

You draw on your own expertise, wisdom and personal experience to cover the important elements of the topic. Your conjectures go beyond the immediate circumstances, to get to deeper truths. You expect the audience to keep up, but will clarify where needed.

Intensity of Sage

🌶 Mild	🌶🌶 Medium	🌶🌶🌶 Hot

CURATOR GEEK EXPERT **PROFESSOR** ACADEMIC GURU **DOYEN(NE)**

All of your expertise may come from studying the thinking of others, or it may be that all of your expertise is self-created.

When your research and thinking has mostly been formed from others, select a **curator-sage.** When your insights come from a mix of your own thinking and the thinking of other experts, select a **professor-sage.** When your wisdom is mostly from your own immense experience and research, select a **doyen(ne)-sage.**

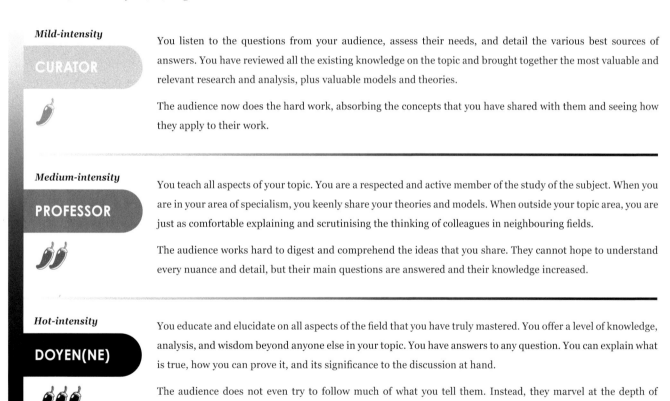

Mild-intensity

CURATOR

🌶

You listen to the questions from your audience, assess their needs, and detail the various best sources of answers. You have reviewed all the existing knowledge on the topic and brought together the most valuable and relevant research and analysis, plus valuable models and theories.

The audience now does the hard work, absorbing the concepts that you have shared with them and seeing how they apply to their work.

Medium-intensity

PROFESSOR

🌶🌶

You teach all aspects of your topic. You are a respected and active member of the study of the subject. When you are in your area of specialism, you keenly share your theories and models. When outside your topic area, you are just as comfortable explaining and scrutinising the thinking of colleagues in neighbouring fields.

The audience works hard to digest and comprehend the ideas that you share. They cannot hope to understand every nuance and detail, but their main questions are answered and their knowledge increased.

Hot-intensity

DOYEN(NE)

🌶🌶🌶

You educate and elucidate on all aspects of the field that you have truly mastered. You offer a level of knowledge, analysis, and wisdom beyond anyone else in your topic. You have answers to any question. You can explain what is true, how you can prove it, and its significance to the discussion at hand.

The audience does not even try to follow much of what you tell them. Instead, they marvel at the depth of analysis and intellectualisation that you share. They are grateful for each profound insight that you provide them with.

 Sage: **Shape Sharpeners**

Tips on how to choose and arrange your content for a sage type of presentation.

Hone Your Messaging

Make your main messages:

wisdoms

Articulate your message in a way that offers a window into the fascinating thinking involved. It should **teach them something** and **grow their knowledge and understanding.**

An insight, explanation, answer, opinion, judgement, interpretation, concept, model.

e.g. *"Those who are not shocked when they first come across quantum theory cannot possibly have understood it."* 1952 Niels Bohr.

Be ready to **repeat** your message multiple times. Find ways to come at your wisdom from different directions. Your audience may not grasp the insights and their significance without this repetition.

Challenge yourself to form your main message into something **visual.** Help your audience to form a viable mental model based on your knowledge – ideally building upon schema they already possess. Turn data into graphs, research methods into diagrams, theories into mind maps, etc.

Shave Your Information

PRIORITISE

The most **relevant** ideas and pertinent **explanations.**

☆ Any **thesis** that offers improved understanding of what happens and why it happens.

☆ Your **interpretation** of the data you have analysed.

INCLUDE

✓ Research results and analysis.

✓ Insights, models.

✓ Theories, axioms and conjectures.

✓ Debates and disagreements.

✓ Alternative perspectives and explanations.

✓ Summary of your interpretation.

DEPRIORITISE

The **simplistic.**

✗ Non-expert ideas or observations.

✗ Content where you have no experience.

✗ Unjustified guesses.

✗ Direction on steps to take.

Great ways to structure parts of your presentation.

Logic Structure – Detective Case:

Structure like the best crime and detective thrillers.

1) Describe the mystery in the form of a puzzle to be solved.

2) Zip through fast analysis of the facts leading to answer one (a total miss).

3) Share obvious evidence that disproves answer one.

4) Slower analysis of the facts building to answer two (a near miss).

5) Share specific evidence that questions answer two.

6) Flash of insight that unlocks final analysis leading to answer three (a hit).

Logic Structure – Subtle Steps:

Loosely based on Aristotle questions.

1) State the question to be answered (perhaps with why it is important).

2) A simplistic answer based on non-expert knowledge, with arguments in favour.

3) Highlight insufficiencies and inaccuracies of the simplistic answer.

4) An expert answer based on greater depth of research and thinking.

5) Pre-emptive responses to likely objections to expert answer.

6) Summary of best overall answer.

Three Structure – Hegel Triangle:

Famous way to bring together opposing explanations into a single improved interpretation of the facts.

1) Thesis – what we believe is true and the evidence for it.

2) Antithesis – examples where the thesis fails and alternative explanations.

3) Synthesis – combining all thinking together to form a combined (and improved) explanation for things.

Great ways to open and close your presentation.

Include in your opening: Set your credibility – the source of your expertise. Carefully articulate the question(s) that you hope to answer in your presentation. This may be a vital request from the business or a general hypothesis or a checklist of queries from the team.

Include in your closing section: Check what outstanding questions remain. Summarise the areas that you have covered. Leave them with a final piece of wisdom.

 Sage: **Shift Keys**

Signal

Indicate to your audience how to listen.

Find a way to show yourself as the expert: your publications, an intro from trusted voice, your work with other experts, the time you invested in studying the topic, biography, etc.

Forewarn your audience that they may not follow everything. Encourage them to ask any questions and to call out when something is confusing. Ascertain if other experts, in your topic area or in a closely connected field, are in the audience. A true sage welcomes alternative perspectives and rich debate.

Spoken Language

Embrace technical language to explain the details of your analysis. Touch on subtleties and nuances in the content, but hold back from going far beyond what **this** audience can follow.

Portray certainty in the rigour of what you say: speak slowly and confidently in theories that you share and opinions that you give. However, be open and excited by alternative explanations. Debate is healthy.

Keep your language precise. The sage avoids hyperbole and other rhetorical devices. Stay within rational explanations for the facts you know and what you believe these facts tell us.

Be comfortable expressing your expert opinion.

Emotional language:

O Probably **keep emotions subdued** / mild.

O Aim emotions towards the ideas that you share: **admiration** for the elegance of the thinking.

Body Language

Your body language may stay fairly reserved. Movements are reasonably measured and slow. The facts and ideas that you share hold sufficient weight – there is no need to flail one's arms around.

Your hands may come up towards your chin in a way similar to Rodin's "The Thinker": you chew a pair of glasses, you stroke your chin, you place your index fingers up to your pursed lips.

You may have limited eye-contact with your audience. You are not being rude; you are preoccupied with ideas. You look up to recall the details of a case study; you frown and gaze at the floor as you scrutinize a specific fact; you shut your eyes as you bring a model to mind.

Overall, you are less interested in your appearance. However, you want to portray intellectual assuredness – colours are likely muted. Dress may be messy, but still smart.

Staging

Ensure your audience can all see your visuals clearly; place most centrally. But create a space for you to be seen with them. You add credibility and credence to the ideas that you share.

You want to be able to see your audience to check if they have questions or to ask them questions.

Keep space to come forward: as you check they understand a vital fact, or to emphasise a primary supposition, deduction, or to share an opinion.

You may stay in one place (in a seat/behind a lectern) or you may enthusiastically move between your content and your audience.

 Virtual: Can you add your webcam into your presentation (e.g. PPT Cameo mode)? Can you set up your webcam so it points towards a flipchart or whiteboard?

 Small room: Get visuals central, but ensure room for you to interact with the content (to point, to guide, to add perspectives).

 Large room: Lecture theatre layout is fine, but consider rows of semi-circles. Can you have multiple displays showing different interpretations?

Visuals

You should utilise whichever visuals best enable you to convey your ideas to your audience: charts, diagrams, models, data tables, quotes, etc.

Nothing needs to be highly designed and refined – it needs to be accurate. Data charts focus on rigour rather than aesthetics. Diagrams may be poorly drawn as long as the meaning is clear.

Visuals should be sufficiently large to represent the intricacies of the content. Sometimes that just means a small screen – but it can be vital to have a very large display where charts and diagrams are complex.

Combine the pre-prepared (e.g. slide deck) and spontaneous (e.g. whiteboard / flip chart).

You may use lots of visuals – spreading the different diagrams and models out across the space. This means any visual can be referenced again quickly.

Look for objects and props that can help you explain your ideas. Can you demonstrate the outcome of a standard experiment? Can you teach a fundamental insight through a 3D model?

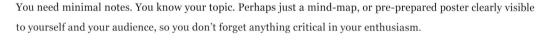

How To Manage Your Presenter Notes

You need minimal notes. You know your topic. Perhaps just a mind-map, or pre-prepared poster clearly visible to yourself and your audience, so you don't forget anything critical in your enthusiasm.

That said, if you do decide to check more detailed notes (e.g. to check specifics of a case study within one of your publications), take your time. What matters is the accurate and full articulation – your audience will wait as you go to your laptop to find the definitive research result that best answers their question.

Interact

You expect the audience to concentrate hard as they learn. You will ask questions to check they understand. You expect them to ask clarification questions where needed. You encourage some creative thinking, but you maintain authority on the topic and flow.

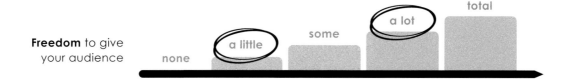

Freedom to give your audience

You will offer more freedom to more experienced people in the audience: their perspectives, their interpretations, their experiences. You welcome natural discussion and debate where they have contributions to make.

Therefore:

O Brief the audience at the start on how and when you want them to share questions (e.g. ask as you go along or hold them to the end of sections) and how they should signal when they are confused.

O Regularly check that they are keeping up. Provide opportunities for the audience to seek clarification.

O Plan in longer sections where the audience is encouraged to ask you questions. Maybe have someone act as an intermediary (e.g. an interviewer).

How? *Example processes include:*

O Build in quizzes to check knowledge - *"Please raise your hand if you believe the answer is 83cm"*

O Directly question volunteers (victims?!) to check knowledge - *"Ahmed, which of these is the right answer: 81, 82, or 83cm?"*

O Lead an "open-audience" Q&A - *"I'd like to invite questions from the audience."*

O Be interviewed - *"Martina, I believe you have sourced a set of questions that you and the audience would like me to address. What would you like to ask me first?"*

Ready Yourself

☐ It's important to make sure you have everything technically ready to share your ideas. Is there enough paper on the flip chart; enough chalk for the blackboard? Are the audio speakers for the research video working properly?

☐ Check the experience level of your audience – what do they grasp already and what is going to be beyond them? What do they need from you today? Be clear on the scope of the advice and expertise that you will limit yourself to.

Sage Prez-type **Watch Outs!**

Beware the dark side of the sage prez-type. Avoid:

Convoluted Oversharing

Avoid going into excessive detail irrelevant and unhelpful to the audience. A few extra facts can be interesting, too many causes confusion (and boredom).

Bubble Talker

Do not get so lost in your fascination in the topic that you ignore your audience completely. Find ways to connect to, and interact with, your audience.

Handling likely objections: An audience can be intimidated by a sage – fearful of questioning an expert. This means concerns and objections can be unspoken. Encourage basic questions, reward people who say *"I do not understand"*, and welcome counter-arguments. Analyse why they are confused, then explain the concepts better.

Sage Prez-type **Powerful Pairings**

  Embody the **sage** prez-type to work through the knowledge and insights that you cover. Your content is complex and detailed so from time to time jump briefly into the **jester** prez-type: share fun facts, make humorous observations, poke fun at your audience.

 Start as the **sage** prez-type – teach the knowledge that the audience needs to know. Then jump into being the **lover** prez-type – make the audience confident in their ability to understand the knowledge.

  As the **ruler** prez-type, define the questions that must be answered. Hop into the **sage** prez-type to analyse the question and come to a considered answer. You may return to be the **ruler** prez-type to communicate the resulting actions to be taken.

 Tricky Transitions: Moving between **sage** prez-type and **caregiver** prez-type or **maverick** prez-type will disrupt their focus on thinking. Your audience wants to access your deep knowledge and profound understanding; they don't want help to form their own inferior theories (**caregiver**) or to have the established theories undermined (**maverick**).

Explorer

As an **explorer** prez-type you drive curiosity and chart discovery.

Explorer

scout

pathfinder

surveyor

adventurer

pioneer

visionary

trailblazer

As an explorer-type presenter you enthusiastically highlight to your audience **new experiences** and **new discoveries**. There is always more to see and more to learn.

You inspire your audience to **stretch into new places**. You open their eyes to new answers, take them deeper into profound understanding. Your audience is transformed by the experience, swept forward by the **sense of adventure**.

The **Essence** of the Explorer

> *"The voyage of discovery is not in seeking new landscapes but in having new eyes."*
> Proust

From Fiction: Our stories are full of key characters who go on long adventures, but which characters are truly adventurous? Who are the people who explore simply for the sense of freedom that this brings them.

Some are travellers. Phileas Fogg racing *Around the World In 80 days*. Captain Kirk travelling through space to *"boldly go where no man has gone before!"* Alice falling down the rabbit hole and eagerly exploring the strange world she finds.

Some are investigators. Dana Scully in *The X-Files* examining supernatural occurrences. Agatha Christie's supersleuth Miss Marple accumulating evidence for later sage-like analysis.

Some are experimenters – testing the outer limits of thinking. Victor Frankenstein experimenting with how to create life. Doc Brown from *Back To The Future* finding ways to travel through time.

From Real World: Some of the best market insights presentations have been delivered by bold explorers. The speaker may rarely travel in a literal sense. They spend their time at their desk slaloming through quantitative data and in focus groups listening attentively to consumers. However, when they stand to speak to us, they enthral with exciting adventure. Their enthusiasm is infectious as they highlight observations, share real examples, spotlight potentially relevant facts.

These people take their audience on an adventure of discovery. They drive their audience across great swathes of content and yet manage to ensure the most novel and interesting moments are charted for future analysis.

Being your explorer prez-type enables your audience to **discover new information** and see existing thinking from a new perspective. Your **eagerness to explore** gives them the freedom to do the same. By bringing them **along on your journey**, you help them see new things first hand, convincing them far more than any abstract explanation is likely to.

Explorer: **When to Select**

Choose to be an explorer prez-type when you want to share your adventure with your audience through your content, and discover new ideas and perspectives.

Select the explorer prez-type when you want to...

...introduce a new trend to a resistant audience.	You have completed a research project and uncovered an emerging trend. Your business team are focussed on the existing plan, so you expect them to initially reject your findings. You help them discover for themselves the implications of your research and the opportunities that come from them.	*e.g. You have identified that the brand's consumers are starting to shift their viewing habits, likely diluting the effectiveness of the marketing plan. We need to shift our marketing operations.*
...make a proposal.	You have a plan that you think a key client (internal or external) will see as a good fit. You want to check their interest in the idea. You share with them what you were looking for in the plan, what you discovered as you explored the options, and the unique elements that you found along the way.	*e.g. You work in corporate communications responsible for the organisation's reputation. You identify a growing social media platform which has a great fit with your consumer base.*
...get observations on a draft.	You have written a progress summary for a project you lead. Before forming a final version, you want to get input from people you trust. As you walk through your summary you regularly pause to ask what they see.	*e.g. You are completing your report on implications for changes in EU laws. You present the draft version to a small group of lawyers, asking for their input.*
...skim across a lot of content.	You have a lot of information to cover. You want to avoid going too deep on any one sub-area. You set the expectation that you will travel at speed across the topics, pausing only briefly for questions. You regularly remind them of how far through the journey they have travelled (and the areas we still need to travel through).	*e.g. You are presenting to the leadership team the findings of the recent employee satisfaction scores. You know they will want to stop and study each chart, but you need them to make notes for later and keep moving forward.*

Explorer **Task:** You are there to...

Check that you can focus on the right thing. The explorer prez-type is best when you want to...

...adventure »

You **adventure** across the landscape of your topic. You **adventure** onwards into unknown paths and territories. You **adventure** forward, impatient for the next experience.

...discover »

You **discover** new information. You **discover** new evidence and thinking. You **discover** new ways of interpreting things, a change in perspective.

As you adventure through your content, and encourage your audience to discover new things, you may consider one or more of the following:

experience »

You engage directly with the topic, looking to get as close to an authentic account as you can. You bring your audience forward to feel involved in your content. You want them to see it and touch it and smell it. Only by experiencing things for themselves will they truly see what is there.

survey »

You map the territory, full of curiosity in what you will find. You collect evidence as you go, you briefly document findings, yet you stay keen to keep moving (deeper analysis can wait). You take snapshots, store objects of interest, note down observations. You sketch out the resulting map, marking down what you find and where you find it.

experiment »

You explore as you go and test what you find. You give your audience the freedom to do the same. You try things in new ways. You test new paths. You are optimistic, confident that there will be as much value found in the journey as there will in the destination.

realise »

You transform their thinking. Your journey brings revelations that add to your audience's understanding. You help them to re-evaluate how they see the world around them.

Intensity of Explorer

 Mild Medium Hot

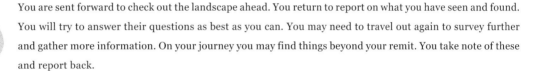

SCOUT   PATHFINDER   SURVEYOR   **ADVENTURER**   PIONEER   VISIONARY   **TRAILBLAZER**

Your explorer prez-type is there to take the audience on a journey of discovery, but how radical the experience is will vary.

When the scope of your discovery is very specific and quite limited, select a **scout-explorer**. When you are far freer to choose your own path, select an **adventurer-explorer**. When your journey is truly pioneering and the implications will set a whole new direction of thinking, select a **trailblazer-explorer**.

Mild-intensity
SCOUT

You are sent forward to check out the landscape ahead. You return to report on what you have seen and found. You will try to answer their questions as best as you can. You may need to travel out again to survey further and gather more information. On your journey you may find things beyond your remit. You take note of these and report back.

Your audience learns new things from your discoveries. They have probably been involved in defining where you have searched. They will certainly have agency over what you share with them on your return.

Medium-intensity
ADVENTURER

You are free to follow where your curiosity takes you. You choose where to explore next, whether to go down side paths or to stick to the original trail, or to set off confidently into an unexplored valley. You are eager to absorb everything you come across, while determined to keep moving forward.

The audience is excited by your discoveries and interesting things that you have found along the way. The experience brings them new evidence, possibilities and perspective.

Hot-intensity
TRAILBLAZER

You are continuously breaking new ground, finding new discoveries, unearthing new revelations. You are going places no one has been before. You have the potential to find ideas and solutions that are breathtaking in nature and breakthrough in impact.

The audience is inspired to see a topic from a new and different perspective. They are swept along by your pioneering spirit: your optimism in finding a radically new piece of information, a novel solution, a profound shift in thinking.

 # Explorer: **Shape Sharpeners**

Tips on how to choose and arrange your content for an explorer type of presentation.

Hone Your Messaging

Make your main messages:

revelations

Information that is new and breakthrough in some way. You are **highlighting the discoveries and the implications that these may bring.**

Discoveries, findings, novelties, eurekas, breakthroughs, curiosities, lightbulb moments.

e.g. *"We have discovered the secret of life."* Francis Crick (announcing the discovery of the structure of DNA to the patrons of the Eagle Pub, Cambridge – February 1953.)

Help your audience to **visualise** your journey. Paint a picture of where you will explore, then mark where you have been and what you have discovered. Share a map of the quest being undertaken, the challenges and the joys. Represent the treasures found.

Convey the **emotion** you experienced on your journey and the passion and excitement you have for what you have discovered. Promise riches, or new understanding, or further meaning, over the brow of each mountain. Highlight what will be, or has been, unearthed through the adventure.

Shave Your Information

PRIORITISE

The most exciting **discoveries** and how they **transform** our understanding.

☆ Content that allows them to **experience** the journey.

☆ The **newest information** that shifts their perspective.

INCLUDE

✓ Maps, diagrams and routes.

✓ Details of what you have found; both good and bad.

✓ Optional side paths.

✓ Brief overviews, summaries.

✓ Experiments, interactions.

✓ Qualitative research.

✓ Rough quantitative data.

DEPRIORITISE

The **known**.

✗ Existing facts and established ideas.

✗ Boring details.

✗ Restricted boundaries.

✗ Strict routes and paths.

Chart Your Structure

Great ways to structure parts of your presentation.

Story Structure – Epic Journey:

Craft a story that takes a hero across a long adventure to new places and experiences, and eventually returns them back to where they started.

1) **Pack the Rucksack:** bring together everything that you need before you set off.

2) **First Fresh Discoveries:** step outside the base and feel the excitement of initial small finds. Let the enjoyment of discovery pull you forward.

3) **Fun Side Paths:** allow branching tracks to lead you away from the planned route. Enjoy the freedom to choose each turn and embrace each new experience.

4) **Major Discoveries:** a mix of serendipity and common sense leads you to important findings. These discoveries may also start you towards new realisations.

Open Structure – Branching Paths:

Craft a network through your content with multiple points where there is a choice on where to go next.

As you approach each fork in the road, pause to choose which path to take – probably allowing your audience significant agency. You may encourage certain choices, as you aim to keep the audience moving towards a desired goal, but mostly you let the audience decide each path.

One Structure – A Grail Quest (MacGuffin):

You have a specific quest – everything is measured against progress towards this goal.

This drives you to travel over large distances. Over time, certain discoveries (examples, data, facts, etc.) become more significant. Some experiences (case studies, anecdotes, discussions, etc.) change our sense of what matters most. You have failed to find your "grail", yet have discovered so much through the journey

Great ways to open and close your presentation.

Include in your opening: Show your audience a map of the journey they will undertake: where you will start, what you know of the topics you will travel through, and the destination you are aiming for. Pack a metaphorical rucksack: the information and tools that everyone needs to understand before you start.

Include in your closing section: Review the journey that you have completed – where you started, where you went, and the highlights that you found on the way. Discuss what new information has come to light, and how this might change how we see the world.

Explorer: **Shift Keys**

Signal

Indicate to your audience how to listen.

Be clear to your audience that you will be exploring new ground. Paint a picture of the journey. Admit there may be wrong turns and dead ends. Maybe describe the mode(s) of transport we will use (how we will travel through the ideas) and summarise the tools and resources we will bring (e.g. models).

Promise them new discoveries and revelations. Describe passionately the merits of reaching our desired destination and the valuable things we will find along the way.

Spoken Language

Ensure your language is visual and optimistic. Language that paints a picture of the information that you cover. Words that articulate hope and aspiration to discover new things.

Summarise what you can see – charting it for future consideration. Eagerly highlight anything that looks novel or new. When you do, pause to talk about it from multiple angles, varied perspectives.

You will often use the metaphor of travel. You will talk of places, landscapes, paths, sidetracks, etc.

Emotional language:

O Be **curious** about everything new that you come across. Feel the **anticipation** for the potential revelation that each discovery will bring you.

O You may, at times, be **impatient** to move on. Deeper analysis can be done back at base – for now you keep moving forward.

Body Language

You are likely to keep moving; after all, you are going on a journey. Try not to be restricted by a pedestal, chair or fixed microphone.

Your body language is likely to be very open as you move across topics; head high to ensure you can see everything well. Each time you discover something of note you move to get the best view of it you can.

Your gestures should guide the attention of the audience e.g. a beckoning motion towards a point of interest. Or you emphasise the direction of travel e.g. a finger pointing across the stage.

Your clothing is likely to be relaxed, reflecting your need to move freely. It should be chosen to be practical for the journey you are going on. Explorers travel in rugged shoes with a rucksack packed with provisions (not heels and a designer computer bag).

Staging

Create a sense of space and freedom to explore. Move across the space, pausing to highlight major discoveries.

Visuals

Share a visual diagram of the areas that you will cover, a map of your content.

Spread your visuals and materials around the room. It is OK to ask your audience to move (e.g. move their seat) to get a better view. Make sure it is easy for potential volunteers to enter the stage, to experience elements of your journey, or inspect your discoveries.

Use topic zones: set an area of the space for each sub-topic. You move to that area of the space as you move to that topic zone. Maybe sequence these in steps from "start" on one side to the "goal" on the other.

Virtual: Find ways to create a sense of movement e.g. move between content; change webcam position.

Small room: Can you turn the table into a space that you travel across, using objects and handouts?

Large room: Maximise the space you have. Plan to use every square inch of the stage. Can you walk into the audience?

Make visuals as large as you can. Think of an old style large map laid out on a table. How do you create this sense of scale?

Use visuals to give a panoramic, bird's eye view of your topic. Use map-like diagrams: schematics, flowcharts, organograms, topic maps, etc. Clearly mark where you are trying to get to, the path taken so far, and major milestones along the way. Return to it often.

When using visuals to highlight findings, zoom into the detail with photos, videos, etc. Find a way to store these pictures in your figurative rucksack – where you can grab them later to review with fresh eyes and compare with other discoveries.

Explorers may bring souvenirs back from their journeys and these can make the most wonderful props to make your journey very real to the audience.

The details will come from your spoken words; avoid including lots of text on your slides.

How To Manage Your Presenter Notes

Make your notes public – visible to your audience. You are leading them on an epic journey of discovery, so you have a map. You refer to this regularly as you track progress. You track for yourself when you are travelling over known ground and when you are stepping into new areas.

You will find many new things as you travel. You may add quite detailed reports on what is found, where it is found, and early thoughts on its significance. Have these well indexed so you can highlight new realisations as you come across them.

Interact

You want your audience to feel the exhilaration and freedom of exploration.

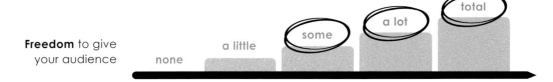

Freedom to give
your audience

none   a little   some   a lot   total

You will be interested in their response to each thing you discover. You might give them a say in when to pause, to investigate further, and where we go next. However, you may want to keep a modicum of control and to ensure you maintain forward progress.

Therefore:

O Plan moments to pause, review progress, and consider where to go next.

O Check how the audience is responding to what you have found. Do they see it too? Have they seen this before – is it new? Do they agree it is important? Should it be documented?

O Encourage your audience to share what they are seeing. Open a space for them to be the first to discover things.

How? *Example processes include:*

O Ask your audience what they are seeing - *"What do you notice in the data?"*

O Encourage open questions from the audience throughout - *"Has anyone experienced this themselves?"; "What do you think our options are?"*

O Invite a moderator to source questions and interview you about the things that you hoped to find and the things that you have discovered - *"I have questions from the audience, but let me start with a question I am keen to ask you..."*

Ready Yourself

☐ Visualise your journey and you moving through it. Bring to mind things you want to highlight. Feel your excitement at the discoveries you will soon share.

☐ Remind yourself of your timings – review when you aim to reach key waypoints through the presentations. Times when you must stop exploring and move on.

☐ Do a physical warm-up that focusses on gentle stretches – you want to be fluid in your movements. Walk the stage area. Go for a walk around the block.

☐ Do an awareness broadening activity. "Find a _____". Pick something to find in your surroundings e.g. find something square; find something blue; find something heavy.

☐ Pack your case of tools: map, pointer, pens, speaker – whatever you might need.

Explorer Prez-type **Watch Outs!**

Beware the dark side of the explorer prez-type. Avoid:

Aimless Wanderer	Greener Grass
Don't go off exploring when it's not needed. Sometimes it is right to stand still, to set up camp where you are, and to make the most out of what you already know.	Make sure your drive for discovery isn't clouding your judgement of the value of what you already know, or the potential costs of the path you are embarking upon.

Handling likely objections: You need to remember that the ambiguous hope of discovery is not enough for all situations. An audience wants to be convinced that the journey will be worth the costs involved, that the potential gains in knowledge outweigh the uncertainty of whether you will find anything new.

Explorer Prez-type **Powerful Pairings**

  As the **everyman** prez-type, acknowledge the limits of present traditions and lay out a need for discovery. Then, as the **explorer** prez-type, travel eagerly through new ideas and discoveries. Finally, return to the **everyman** prez-type to summarise learnings.

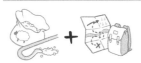 Start as the **caregiver** prez-type – you make sure they have what they need to stay safe on the journey. Once everyone is ready jump into the **explorer** prez-type to help them explore: highlight things of interest, take surprising turns, pronounce discoveries.

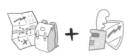 You begin as the **explorer** prez-type, enjoying the freedom to roam through content, discovering as you go. At some point this leads to a moment of danger – you hop into **hero** prez-type to convince them of the need to persevere.

 Tricky Transitions: Moving between **explorer** prez-type and **jester** prez-type or **ruler** prez-type can confound your audience. They want you to get the right balance between safety and freedom; they don't want to risk losing their way through foolishness (**jester**) or be too constrained by predefined controls (**ruler**).

Hero

As a **hero** prez-type you convey a compelling cause and inspire commitment.

Hero

accidental

volunteer

proponent

champion

defender

campaigner

superhero

As a hero-type presenter you believe passionately in a "just cause", a "noble endeavour". **You have absolute certainty it is worth pursuing**. You shoulder the greatest risks, **determined to overcome any challenges**, despite the dangers.

The audience is exhilarated by your bravery. They admire your resolve and are **convinced of the need for action**. They are **inspired to be courageous**, to take on new challenges.

The **Essence** of the Hero

From Fiction: We are all used to heroes in the plethora of stories we enjoy, but do we really stop and think about what makes them "heroic"? What is the essence of the quintessential hero that is consistent across the characters as diverse as James Bond, Eliza Doolittle (*My Fair Lady*), Captain America (*Marvel*), Mirabel Madrigal (*Encanto*), Katniss Everdeen (*The Hunger Games*), Harry Potter, or Andy Dufresne (*The Shawshank Redemption*)?

In every story the hero is courageous, prioritising a just endeavour, accepting the risks to their own welfare. This "just endeavour" can vary from saving the world (Bond), saving her family (Mirabel), inspiring a revolution (Katniss) or maintaining dignity and hope in the face of a corrupt regime (Andy). The "risks" can be expulsion from the family, or injustice, or personal harm.

The hero has an ethos: bravery, spirit, character. The hero steps forward as others step back. The hero accepts dangers because success is vital.

> *"He who has a why to live for can bear almost any how."*
> Friedrich Nietzsche

From Real World: A hero fits naturally when the stakes are high. For example, the general manager at the yearly away day who shares the existing business struggles and lays out the importance of a new business strategy. Or a charity leader who describes the vital nature of the work they do for the community in particular, and for society in general.

Still, a hero can be appropriate for less lofty occasions. Perhaps, a finance manager needs a team to take the invoicing processes more seriously – they cannot convince them of the "joys" of invoicing best practice, but they can emphasise the ethics of doing the right thing for the business as a whole.

Being your hero prez-type **inspires your audience to put aside concerns** (and risks), dismiss a temptation for inaction, and embrace a vital cause. You passionately persuade your audience to believe in the mission. You are impatient to get started, every fibre of your being **driven by a predilection for action**. This stirs the same in your audience.

 Hero: **When to Select**

Choose to be a hero prez-type presenter when you need to convince a group of the need for change. You want them to see your courage to act as an inspiration for them to follow.

Select the hero prez-type when you want to...

... persuade people of the merits of a new strategy.	You have a new strategy for the team, with a new direction and new challenges. You need them to recognise the significance of this change, to stop and take note. And you need them to ardently believe in the importance of the new strategy.	*e.g. You take the whole team off-site for a major strategy day. You are setting up the day with the opening speech – setting the tone.*
...rally people to get started.	You need to get people to begin, but in a situation where many aspects are new: new team, new roles, new industry, new initiative, etc. There is no efficient way to make every step ahead clear and easy, so to break the inertia, you inspire people to commence the work and to learn as we go.	*e.g. You bring the eco-team together in the office. You highlight how we are suffering from analysis paralysis – only talking about options for action. It is time to stop analysing and to get started.*
...encourage a leadership team to make a difficult decision.	You need a leadership team to make a vital business decision. You have laid out to them all the evidence for and against the decision. You suspect they are prolonging discussions and stalling on making a choice, but the decision cannot wait. You need them to prioritise making a judgement.	*e.g. A colleague has completed a presentation outlining a key dilemma. You step forward to give a brief speech on the imperative to decide and act now. We can wait no longer.*
...motivate a team to put aside personal concerns.	You are aware that your audience is worried. There is jeopardy involved, and although you can mitigate for some, there are tangible risks. You need people to feel that the mission is worth any potential danger, and trust that you will shoulder the greatest burden and take on the greatest challenges.	*e.g. You are presenting a plan that delays the key initiative launch by six months. The sales teams are nervous that their customers and clients will be very angry. They are correct, but this is still the right course of action.*

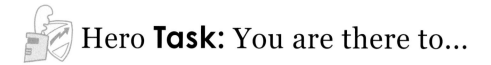# Hero **Task:** You are there to…

Check that you can focus on the right thing. The hero prez-type is best when you want to…

…convince »

You **convince** them of the importance of the mission.
You **convince** them that doing nothing is foolhardy.
You **convince** them that we must do the right thing.

…inspire »

You **inspire** them to accept the mission. You **inspire** them to step courageously towards any danger. You **inspire** them to be determined and steadfast to the end.

As you convince them of the importance and inspire them to act, concentrate on one or more of the following:

strive »

You persist through grit and determination. Be resolute throughout. You are pushing yourself to your limits (of intelligence, of skill, of effort, of bravery, etc.) to move towards your final goal. Giving up is simply not an option.

risk »

You accept the dangers. You freely acknowledge your personal worries and concerns – you are not a fool, you recognise the risks – but you have measured them against the value of success (and the pain of failure). You are aware of the potential for personal injury or loss, but you step forward anyway. Needs must!

believe »

You feel what you feel. You maintain your intense faith in the purpose of your undertaking. Something inherently important is at stake, and you have complete conviction in what must be achieved and why it must be achieved. There is not even a scintilla of doubt – only certainty of spirit.

manoeuvre »

You are skilful, you improvise, you are quick witted and creative in the moment. What matters is the outcome, which leads you to use any (legal and ethical) means at your disposal. A shortcut may be needed. An imperfect solution may suffice to overcome a pressing problem. Whatever it takes!

Intensity of Hero

 Mild
 Medium
 Hot

ACCIDENTAL VOLUNTEER PROPONENT **CHAMPION** DEFENDER CAMPAIGNER **SUPERHERO**

As a hero you may be the last person in the room expected to step up or you may be the obvious choice.

When you are no different to anyone else, select an **accidental-hero**. When you are a natural choice within this group to take a stand for what is right, aim into the middle of this prez-type, and select a **champion-hero**. When you are the only choice, imbued with powers beyond anyone else, transform into your **super-hero**.

Mild-intensity

You were simply in the right/wrong place in the right/wrong time. It could have been any of us, but fate meant it was you. You bring no special talent (strength, intellect, experience, etc.) to events. Through bravery, pluck, and a noble spirit, you find ways to overcome every challenge.

You inspire the audience to realise that if you can take action, they can too.

Medium-intensity

CHAMPION

Your audience chose you as the person best placed to take on these challenges. You are the strongest, the most capable, or the one who most intensely believes in the imperative of the situation. You accept their trust in you with humility and honour. You put your whole mind and body into accomplishing what needs to be accomplished.

You lead everyone towards each challenge, being first to every obstacle. Through your bravery you inspire others to follow close behind you.

Hot-intensity

SUPERHERO

You are unique. You are capable of things that no one else is. You are the only logical choice to take on the challenges and to achieve the vital goals.

Initially, they see you as impervious to harm and certain of success. They do not realise that you have a weakness too (even Superman has Kryptonite!). Something connected to this scenario is putting you in some form of jeopardy.

The audience realises that even someone imbued with such power is taking personal risk. This inspires them to do the same.

 Hero: **Shape Sharpeners**

Tips on how to choose and arrange your content for a hero type of presentation.

Hone Your Messaging

Make your main messages:

endeavours

You want to set out **what needs to be achieved**, possibly with a sense of what will **happen if we fail**.

That is:

A mission, enterprise, venture, goal, quest, cause, target.

e.g. *"Working together to end poverty and injustice"* Oxfam.

Challenge yourself to find words with heightened **emotion**. Perhaps articulate the intense pride which will be felt when we achieve a noble goal. Or describe the sense of abject despair that will be felt if we fail.

Draw a vivid picture of what success or failure will deliver. Turn a target number into a finishing line on a tracking chart on the wall. Transform an abstract goal (*"$12 million sales"*) into a human outcome (*"clean water for one million households"*).

Shave Your Information

PRIORITISE

Outcomes to be achieved, and propelling **actions**.

☆ **Information on the goal:** what it is, why it is vital, and our progress towards it.

☆ **The bad outcomes** that will transpire if we do not act.

INCLUDE

✓ Content that describes the personal risks involved.

✓ Personal (figurative) injuries endured.

✓ Content regarding a known adversary/nemesis.

✓ Shrewd and inventive solutions to a challenge.

✓ Personal stories.

✓ Lessons learnt.

DEPRIORITISE

The **intellectual**.

✗ Detailed plans except for the present challenge.

✗ Detailed analysis during the action.

✗ Personal gain, glory, excitement.

Great ways to
structure parts of
your presentation.

Three Structure – Three Act Story:

Craft a traditional epic tale with a central protagonist. Below is a guiding recipe. It can be the basis of an exciting anecdote as well as for a serious data presentation.

1) **Situation:** set the scene, introduce a central likeable protagonist, share their hopes and fears.

2) **Complication:** introduce a primary objective and obstacle(s). Vividly describe the challenge and the creative actions taken to overcome it.

3) **Resolution:** describe the new world – much is the same but something has changed.

One Structure – Sole Raison d'être:

Where the goal is of such profound import, it can be the central tenet of key sections of your presentation. If it matters enough, it can be all that matters. Every piece of information is solely considered and judged against achieving the critical outcome. Connect everything to the central endeavour.

Two Structure – Opposing Pairs:

The hero is regularly battling as the "good" against the "bad". Their good intent against the selfishness of another. Their kindness against another's cruelty. The easy path to anguish in contrast to the hard path to triumph. The potential future if we succeed, against the certain future if we fail.

Great ways to
open and close
your presentation.

Include in your opening: Lay out the goal to be achieved and the likely challenges along the way. Spend some time describing the context – the scope of the domain you are talking about. Your goal should feel vital within this context (e.g. launching your initiative on time is probably trivial within the context of world hunger, but can feel crucial within the lives of this team).

Include in your closing section: Highlight how we will feel when we succeed: pride, relief, joy, etc. Focus praise on others or the collective. Downplay your role (your personal gain and your personal injury). Focus on how things will return to commonplace routines. Ideally bring back an idea or content included in the opening but not referenced since (technically a "reintegration").

Hero: **Shift Keys**

Avoid bravado and self-promotion! In fact, look to signal the opposite: embody humility and selflessness. Reference or show a simple kindness. Acknowledge but disregard the risks to you personally. All that matters is the path towards a noble objective.

Once the goal is set, demonstrate a propensity for action (i.e. move quickly on to the first challenge). Maybe introduce a nemesis; paint them as mean spirited and ignoble.

Spoken Language

Prioritise language around values like: truth, character, integrity, and doing the right thing for the right reasons.

Be comfortable using first person "I" when explaining the most dangerous actions. Vividly describe the challenges as you come across them and the deeds taken to overcome them.

Keep descriptions and information in a standard language – so the audience can easily see themselves in each situation.

Emotional language:

O Be open to expressing any **sadness** and **anger** you feel for injustices, unfairness, dangers to others.

O **Anticipate** the relief you will feel when you succeed.

Body Language

Stand tall and open. You are confident and eager.

Make your gestures demonstrative – literally showing and emphasising the challenges, the risks, and the actions taken.

Arms are most often loose and agile. But your hands are available (ready to reach for a shield or sword). You will show strength (and resolve) when needed.

You are dressed ready for action. You are likely unencumbered – the hero did not take the time to pack everything needed e.g. jacket off and shirt sleeves rolled up.

Staging

You enter confidently onto the "stage" – you are eager to get started.

Start and end in the centre of the space – ensure you have everyone's attention. You may stay there throughout, or you may move as you talk of each challenge.

Ideally you stand tall, ready to move in any direction. Perhaps stand with one foot slightly in front of the other and knees slightly bent – ready to act.

If possible, keep some separation between you and the audience (including before the presentation) so your entrance has impact.

Virtual: Can you add your webcam into your presentation (e.g. PPT Cameo mode)? Can you set up your webcam so it points towards a flipchart or whiteboard?

Small room: Get visuals central, but ensure room for you to interact with the content (to point, to guide, to add perspectives).

Large room: Lecture theatre layout is fine, but consider rows of semi-circles. Can you have multiple displays showing different interpretations?

Visuals

You may not even need any visuals. You could be your primary visual tool.

Photos depicting the importance of the just cause, the obstacles, the successes, the prizes along the way. Visuals may show some aspects in unsettling detail – the "dragon" needs to look dangerous and strong.

Most visuals can look basic in terms of design. You are focussed on saving the day rather than slide templates and high design.

Something may symbolise the cause being fought for e.g. a talk on climate change may show a single polar bear whose ongoing existence is uncertain.

Visualise or represent the enemy, the nemesis that you are competing against (ideally placed to one side of the stage).

If something is won, treasure of some sort, this should be brought into the room – shared first and foremost with the audience.

How To Manage Your Presenter Notes

Ideally, talk without notes. The hero survives despite being poorly prepared, relying on tenacity and courage. Presenting without notes is a high wire act fraught with danger i.e. it is the heroic thing to do.

The exception may be notes written by others; something integral to solving a key challenge (e.g. the insight data from the research team that you stumbled upon and that proved the key to solving the marketing challenge).

Interact

You probably want to give the audience some freedom, because they need to get involved in the change you are striving for. You do not want to offer complete freedom, because you need them focussed on your single objective.

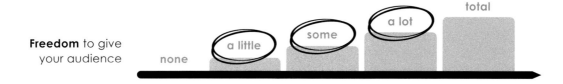

Freedom to give your audience

So you are moving between giving the audience a little and a lot of freedom.

Therefore:

○ Use rhetorical devices that engage an audience but keep them listening.

○ Encourage group creativity in ways of overcoming each challenge, but the ultimate goal must not change.

○ Be ready to reward all moments where the audience shows heroism (bravery, courage, ethos, tenacity, etc.).

How? *Example processes include:*

○ Check-step questions to the audience to confirm they agree that the quest is essential and necessary: *"I see no other option other than to find a way to pause the launch. Do you agree?"*

○ Use rhetorical questions: *"I ask myself, who has been in this situation before? Who can offer us advice or an alternative? And the answer that comes to mind is..."*

○ Encourage them to help find innovative solutions to each problem but keep control of the path towards the goal.

○ After the core presentation offer an open Q&A: the audience asks you questions: *"Now that you have heard the full story, what questions do you have?"*

Ready Yourself

☐ Spend focussed time reminding yourself of the cause you are fighting for. Be ready to explain to the audience its significance and importance.

☐ Complete a selection of stretching exercises. Stretch key arm and leg muscles. Stretch your back (safely). You want to have heroic energy as you present – ready to "leap into action" if needed.

☐ Stretch your voice through singing exercises. Focus on gently stretching your pitch downwards – determination involves a lower pitched speaking voice.

Hero Prez-type **Watch Outs!**

Beware the dark side of the hero prez-type. Avoid:

The Egotist

Avoid self-publicity and self-congratulation. Being heroic is seen as a positive trait only up to a point. Your focus is on the endeavour; it must <u>not</u> be about you.

Thrill Seeker

The personal risk must be justifiable in relation to the outcome. The audience may be thrilled, but your reaction should be relief and not euphoria.

Handling likely objections: They may demand more clarity. *"We need to know about challenges we will face. We need to check whether we have the capabilities needed. We need to be certain about the risks."* Acknowledge these hesitancies, admit you were tempted to pause, but highlight why action must be taken now and must be taken by us.

Hero Prez-type **Powerful Pairings**

Start as the **hero** prez-type to get straight into the action – solving problems and overcoming challenges. At some point determination and courage is not enough. Skip into **sage** prez-type to bring in important experience and wisdom, providing the key to solve a major obstacle. Then skip back to **hero** again.

Start as the **everyman** prez-type, a person similar to anyone in the room. Then let events unfold (your content flow) such that you are left with no option other than to stand up and step up, transforming into a **hero** prez-type.

Start as the **hero** prez-type, setting out the noble undertaking that will take grit and bravery from us all. Once you arrive at the first major obstacle, jump into **ruler** prez-type to confidently "martial your troops" (define roles, set expectations, co-ordinate priorities).

Tricky Transitions: Moving between **hero** prez-type and **lover** prez-type or **creator** prez-type can lead to perilous inconsistencies. All that matters to you is the endeavour you are undertaking. This leaves insufficient devotion for either your audience (**lover**) or your plan (**creator**).

Magician

As a **magician** prez-type you attest that the impossible is now possible.

Magician

conjurer

wiz

technologist

oracle

inventor

visionary

sorcerer

As a magician-type presenter you do something that **amazes the audience**. You demonstrate that **the thing which seemed painfully hard is now easily possible**. Through your magic (new vision or technology or initiative) everything changes.

The audience reassesses their existing beliefs, **catalysing a paradigm shift**. You have shown them an updated reality, with new possibilities.

The **Essence** of the Magician

From Fiction: There are many fictional characters who are literal magicians, e.g. Merlin from Arthurian legends and the Three Witches from *Macbeth*. Some stories include non-magicians who are capable of truly magical things, e.g. Mary Poppins and Cinderella's Fairy Godmother. Some characters offer powerful, yet opaque, foresights that change a hero's route to the future: Mama Odie (from *The Princess and The Frog*) and The Oracle (from *The Matrix*). Some simply pass on some "magical object" to the hero demanding that they use it wisely and carefully: Q from James Bond and Obi-Wan Kenobi from *Star Wars*.

In all of these stories, this "magic" enables the hero to change direction, either through the foresight they offer or by solving unsolvable challenges.

From Real World: On January 9, 2007, at the Macworld conference in San Francisco, Steve Jobs stepped onto stage to unveil the new iPhone.[23] A global audience watched transfixed as he calmly showed what a true "smartphone" could do.

Go back and watch the first few minutes; you see the magician expertly embodied. Watch his poise as he starts. His sense of occasion – he knows that he is about to change what the world thinks a phone can do and be.

He makes a bold promise for a better future. He surgically cuts to shreds the credibility of existing "smartphones". He promises three breakthrough devices, before quickly promising that these three amazing devices are held in a single device (see "The Prestige Triple" later). He brings out the iPhone and shows it doing amazing things.

Being your magician prez-type inspires your audience to **recalibrate their perception** of reality. Impossible things become possible. Hard things become easy. You are there to demonstrate this new power, but not to explain how it works. **Your audience will feel exceptional**, enabled by the magic you offer. Ensure they are respectful of the responsibility this power brings.

Magician: **When to Select**

Choose to be a magician prez-type when you need people to reconsider what is possible, and you have something transformational to share. You want them to be amazed and energised by what they see.

Select the magician prez-type when you want to...

...persuade them a breakthrough is here.	You want to convince a client or internal stakeholder. You have a pioneering new vision, technology, or service to introduce to them. You know they are sceptical – maybe attempts before have failed. You need to show them that their fears and preconceptions can be dispelled.	*e.g. You are introducing a groundbreaking new product to market. This involves a redesign of the whole category. You need to wow them from the start!*
...demonstrate a capability (without explaining how it works).	You want to impress a stakeholder on a new capability. You want to captivate them in what it does, mesmerise as you demonstrate it in action. However, you do not want to show any of the inner workings – maybe you need them to rely on your service, or you will leave detailed instructions.	*e.g. You are presenting to a major client your powerful in-house data analysis tool. You want your audience to call you back in to discuss how it can help guide their business plans.*
...excite people behind a new strategy.	You have a new business strategy. It means changing an integral aspect of your current business model. You have a "magical element" that will enable the transformation: a new org structure, a new technology, a new consumer insight, etc. With this you can enthral your audience.	*e.g. You are setting the vision for the next fiscal year. The vision involves an innovation beyond all expectations. Everyone is sat, you turn down the lights, and step forward to rock their world.*
...focus attention on very specific elements of an initiative.	You need to highlight elements of a more comprehensive plan. Your story is strongest if they engage mostly with a select few things. You want to distract their attention away from "over there" (topic x), so you add spectacle and pizzazz to captivate them "over here" (topic y).	*e.g. You want alignment for a project. You want to avoid questions on exact timings, so you dazzle them with the exciting new technologies in manufacturing.*

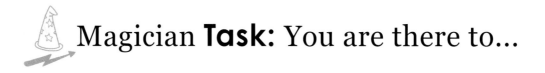

Magician **Task:** You are there to...

Check that you can focus on the right thing. The magician prez-type is best when you want to...

...amaze »

You **amaze** them by promising something improbable. You **amaze** them by demonstrating something impressive. You **amaze** them by revealing something remarkable.

...transform »

You **transform** their perspective in what is possible. You **transform** their ambition in what we can achieve. You **transform** the moment from being commonplace to being a moment of shared optimism.

As you are amazing them and transforming their sense of the possible, concentrate on one or more of the following:

surprise »
You astonish them. You do the unexpected. You may hint towards one thing and then deliver something different. Maybe, if they expect you to pull the rabbit out of the hat, you find a way to reveal a dove.

impress »
You go beyond their wildest expectations. Leave a sense of awe. Create a wow moment. Leave them with an experience that they will talk to each other about for a long time to come. If you asked them to choose a card, don't just pull their card out from the deck, make every other card disappear.

enchant »
You put on a show. Find ways to fascinate them, beguile them, and captivate them. Magic is not done; it is performed. They want a level of theatrics as part of your performance. Use charm, tell stories, add lighting and music. Things that will transfix them.

supercharge »
You enable and energise them. You offer them the opportunity to wield the power you possess. With your oversight, they can now act stronger, think smarter, drive faster or reach further. You flame their optimism and fuel their ambitions.

# **Intensity** of Magician

 Mild   Medium   Hot

CONJURER   WIZ   TECHNOLOGIST   **ORACLE**   INNOVATOR   VISIONARY   **SORCERER**

As a magician you may only add a few parlour tricks, or you may harness power beyond their imagination.

When you can master magic tricks, select a **conjurer-magician**. When you possess true magic but are aware you cannot fully comprehend it, select an **oracle-magician**. If your command of this magic is complete, select a **sorcerer-magician**.

Mild-intensity

CONJURER

You have no magical powers, but you have the skill to enthral and enchant. You add magical theatrics to highlight the most important and impressive elements of your content.

Perhaps your idea is mundane but vital; your audience will thank you for adding spectacle into the performance. Perhaps your information is vast and complex; your audience will appreciate how your whimsical illusions pull their attention to just the most important aspects.

Medium-intensity

ORACLE

You have access to great power (a vision, a technology, a strategy, etc.). You do not pretend to fully understand or fully control this power, but you know how to bring wonder and amazement from what it can do.

Maybe you are the holder of game-changing consumer insights. Maybe you lead the team that brings technical innovations. You are likely to be mysterious as well as impressive, cryptic as well as wise.

Hot-intensity

SORCERER

You wield powerful magic (vision, tech, budget, people, etc.) to a level few others can comprehend. You possess the ability to spellbind, to supercharge, and to transform. If you choose to, you can inspire awe. You see the present without limitations and modify the future.

The audience is enthralled by what you show them.

 Magician: **Shape Sharpeners**

Tips on how to choose and arrange your content for a magician type of presentation.

Hone Your Messaging

Make your main messages:

visions

You want to lead with the promise that something **wonderful and miraculous is now possible.**

A prophecy, a promise, a miracle, a dream, a capability, a power.

e.g. *"1,000 songs in your pocket."* Steve Jobs launching the iPod in 2001.

The outcome that you promise should sound **astonishing**. It should promise something that is almost unbelievable. For it to feel like magic it must deliver something far beyond the everyday.

If work is to be done, it should seem strangely **short** and **simple**. The magician needs only to click their fingers or wave their wand. Your magic is accessed remarkably easily (and strengthened when you are there).

Shave Your Information

PRIORITISE

Things that have **impact** and are **spectacular**.

☆ **Impressive demos:** the most extraordinary things you can show them, ideally that will blow their socks off!

☆ **Outstanding benefits** that are now available to them. Potential business results, team capabilities, breakthrough goals.

INCLUDE

✓ Content that shows the everyday transformed into the special.

✓ Headlines from research or testing that support your claims.

✓ An introduction and overview of where the "magic" comes from.

✓ Routine or ritual for accessing (starting, beginning) the "magic".

DEPRIORITISE

The **how**.

✗ Technical explanations.

✗ Detailed instructions on how to recreate the magic.

✗ Lengthy research analysis.

✗ Anything already easy to achieve.

Great ways to structure parts of your presentation.

Two Structure – A Dawning Double:

Split your content into two clear halves.

1) For the first half, remind the audience of the era just past – with its disappointments and constrictions.

2) For the second half, reveal the magic; highlight how a new era is dawning with reinvigorated abilities and fresh expectations.

Three Structure – The Prestige Triple:

Organise your content as three steps, working through a classic magician's trick performance. To impress people a great deal, it can be good to initially only impress them a little bit.

1) **The pledge:** introduce something mundane. Frame content so it validates the audience's belief that this thing is commonplace and limited.

2) **The turn:** show that it is, in fact, special. It is capable of something surprising and valuable. Demonstrate it achieving something unexpected but not astonishing. Celebrate what this new capability could mean, although hint that we only wish it could do more.

3) **The prestige:** finally, deliver something exponentially more impressive. This is not just special; it is unique and powerful. Lay out the vital things which can be achieved now that this "magic" is with us.

Time Structure – The Potion Recipe:

Slowly step towards the amazing outcome. Methodically add each ingredient and complete each action as you boil your metaphorical cauldron. Each element added, each step taken, moves us closer to the big reveal. Each time an ingredient is added, the potion becomes more vibrant, it bubbles more vigorously, and generally promises greater power.

Great ways to open and close your presentation.

Include in your opening: Your vision, your guarantee for a better today and an even better tomorrow. Offer a glimpse of the magic (and the magic object) you will later unveil, but hold off showing its full power for now. Reference where the magic power will come from.

Include in your closing section: A recap of the main message (the new capability available for us to employ), a bow, and a final flourish (trick).

Magician: **Shift Keys**

Signal

Indicate to
your audience
how to listen.

Start confidently and strongly – this is no time for doubt. Do or say something mysterious – you want the audience to sense something different is going to happen. Hint at the amazing things that they will experience during the presentation.

Maybe mildly disparage the insufficiencies of present capabilities. Reference the normal, highlighting how dull and unimpressive it is.

Spoken Language

Talk slowly and with a sense of wonder. Key phrases may mimic incantations (e.g. nonsense words like "abracadabra").

Talk with simple language but in a slightly quirky way. Strip away dull technical terms. Put everything into common parlance. Tease for the magic to come.

Speak with reverence as you introduce the "magic" to the audience. It is what is impressive; you only harness it.

Look for a rhythm and lyricism to your delivery e.g. as you list the ingredients for your "magic potion".

Then be ready to stop talking as you demo the capabilities of your "magic".

Emotional language:

O Reference your **anticipation** in sharing the "magic" with them...

O ...and feel the joy when you do.

Body Language

Stand (or sit) proudly, front towards your audience. The power of the magic brings you increased sense of worth.

Use gestures to grab and focus attention towards the magic (and away from anything "un-magic"). Move slowly and with control. You are comfortable and in control, although aware you are handling something exciting yet powerful. Treat it with reverence and respect.

When the magic happens, gestures move quicker – to emphasise its power and our wonder.

Maintain control of the source of the power. A volunteer may get to use it, but you keep it close.

Always know what is coming next e.g. when you "click" to next slide don't check it – you know what it shows.

Dress impressively and boldly. Blacks and reds are good. Smart is good. Covered except for your hands (wizards and witches show little flesh!).

Staging

Walk slowly and carefully into the space with a sense of occasion – something awesome is about to occur.

Look for a way to bring a sense of mystery to how the room is laid out e.g. an unusual chair layout, or no chairs at all, or changed lighting, or music.

The powerful "magic" takes centre stage. Arrange the space so you can stand (or sit) just to the side. Create space between the "magic" and your audience, a threshold through which only chosen volunteers pass.

Create a clearly defined route for volunteers to follow to join you. Consider a co-presenter (assistant) to guide volunteers forward or to bring forward the next magic item.

Virtual: Set yourself further back in the camera.
Do not spotlight your webcam, the "magic" is foremost.

Small room: Try to create a small stage space – where everyone can see but no one is too close.

Large room: Explore the use of lighting, music, and technical stage elements to evoke a sense of wonder.

Visuals

Some elements may be deliberately mundane in nature: standard examples of everyday things. Other visuals will be deliberately impressive and vivid.

Find ways to unveil the "magic object". This can be a simple slide transition or sweeping back a red curtain.

Look to impress them in how you visualise the power of your magic e.g. skilfully formed slide animations, technical demonstrations. Add in "magical symbols" – your version of runes and arcane language.

Look for creative ways to bring in props and other objects. Your technical specifications handbook now becomes the spell book for only the qualified to use. Your clicker for moving on to a next slide now becomes the magic wand that will reveal astounding test results.

Demonstrate the magic. Show the magic happening. Show something normal, then show it being better, then show it being something truly amazing/new.

How To Manage Your Presenter Notes

Be very well rehearsed. Everything should feel like it flows naturally while running like clockwork.

Where you need to use notes, do not look to hide them. Do the opposite: treat them like the magical writings of an arcane magic book – reading each page in front of them; or as the usage instructions for the revolutionary new application – projecting them up onto your main screen.

Interact

You give away very little freedom. You may offer a sense of audience choice but, in reality, you have everything meticulously planned out.

Freedom to give your audience

none · a little · some · a lot · total

You are unflappable – aware of the audience but you are unchanged by them. Any "flexing" to their responses is simply an alternative branch within pre-ordained options.

However, you want to involve the audience. This is often through one or more volunteers coming forward to experience the "magic" first-hand. Or it might come from call and response interactions, where everyone is briefly involved.

Therefore:

O Plan carefully a process where you are directly involving volunteers. Work hard to craft clear instructions that restrict their actions to only what you want them to do.

O Use rhetorical questions to maintain control.

O Avoid or park questions on how the magic works. Encourage questions and observations on what the magic now enables us to do differently.

How? *Example processes include:*

O Rhetorical questions – *"Can any of us even imagine analysing and understanding so much data so quickly?"*

O Audience volunteers who show "mere mortals" achieving incredible results through the magician's guiding hand – *"I need someone to come forward and just press this button here..."*

O Show and tell, where the audience must combine the magician's words with the visual spectacle in front of them to comprehend the result – *"Watch what happens when the consumer uses our product for the first time."*

Ready Yourself

☐ Practise, practise, practise. Everything needs to work brilliantly first time and every time. Everything needs to look infallible.

☐ Ensure you do a full warm-up away from the audience. You need to be ready to step forward with confidence and poise from the outset.

Magician Prez-type **Watch Outs!**

Beware the dark side of the magician prez-type. Avoid:

Power-crazed

Avoid being overly thrilled by the amazing capability that you now possess. With power comes responsibility. Be excited, but don't become delirious with this power!

Overreach

Beware promising things that you cannot deliver. You can add sparkle and special effects, but the thing you share needs to be truly amazing in its own right.

Handling likely objections: There will be cynics who doubt the extraordinary. If they doubt the validity of your claims, be ready to demonstrate results in action so they see it with their own eyes. If they doubt whether your magic is any more powerful than other magic, be ready to directly compare your power with the inferior power of competing options.

Magician Prez-type **Powerful Pairings**

Start as the **magician** prez-type to lay out your vision for what is now possible. Then jump to **ruler** prez-type to set targets for delivery and execution – so people know what is expected of them.

Start as the **hero** prez-type to tell the story of how you and others have overcome challenges similar to those we face today. Then hop to **magician** prez-type to introduce the magic item (e.g. vision, tech, or initiative) that enables us to overcome the present challenges.

Start as the **maverick** prez-type to challenge our present thinking and push for why we need to make a change. Then hop to **magician** prez-type to introduce the magic item (e.g. vision, software, or initiative) that will enable us all to make the difficult transition.

Tricky Transitions: Moving between **magician** prez-type and **everyman** prez-type or **student** prez-type can feel jarring to the audience. How can you profess to have unique powers while also having an equal standing to your audience (**everyman**) or an equal level of understanding (**student**).

Maverick

As a **maverick** prez-type you provoke dissatisfaction in the status quo.

Maverick

outsider

provocateur

challenger

reformer

progressive

rebel

revolutionary

As a maverick-type presenter you **challenge the established thinking**. You **spotlight all that is wrong** with existing ideas and practices. Your fresh perspective comes from your **strong values and ethics**.

You **rally people to change their perspective**. When compared to indisputable core principles, sticking to the present thinking would be unconscionable. The audience feels invigorated and exhilarated.

The Essence of the Maverick

From Fiction: Maverick characters bring useful disruption and a sense of cool. They live by their rules; in doing so they break the rules of others. Think Maverick played by Tom Cruise in both *Top Gun* films. Erin Brockovich (Julia Roberts) takes on corporate polluters in her unorthodox way. Lt. Col. Slade in the film of *Scent of a Woman* is a maverick in full flow. In each case, we feel the exhilaration and draw to get involved.

Hans Solo, in *Star Wars*, refuses to live within the constraints of the Empire. Merida, in the film *Brave*, refuses to follow a standard princess's life. These characters exemplify the power of challenging established norms. They act as a catalyst for change in their worlds.

In the true-life film *Hidden Figures*, Kevin Costner plays the (fictionalised) director of the Space Task Group at NASA, Al Harrison. Harrison breaks down racial and gender barriers, to ensure the African-American women in his team, particularly Katherine Johnson, can perform their crucial work. He embodies strong values and a willingness to challenge others.

From Real World: YouTube is full of maverick communicators. Here are examples. Beware, you may not always agree with them:

Sheryl Sandberg's TED Talk on "Why we have too few women leaders".[25] Tim Spector, professor of genetic epidemiology at King's College London, up-ending our understanding of nutrition.[26] Stephen Fry, at the Intelligence Squared event, debating the goodness of the Catholic Church.[27] Mhairi Black, in 2015, elected as the youngest UK Member of Parliament (MP) since 1832, in her maiden speech daring to call out the existing government with the "F-Word".[28]

> *"Progress is impossible without change, and those who cannot change their minds cannot change anything."*
> George Bernard Shaw [24]

Being your maverick prez-type compels your audience to **consider alternative thinking**. You connect them to incontrovertible truths, forcing them to **acknowledge the senselessness of the existing norms**. You highlight the absurd, the anachronistic, and the obsolete. You shake them out of their present inertia. You offer them a vital chance to **truly live by their values**.

 # Maverick: **When to Select**

Choose to be a maverick prez-type when you want to challenge your audience's thinking and rally them behind your distinct ethics and values.

Select the maverick prez-type when you want to...

...challenge a well-established process.	You have identified a problem: your current processes are not leading to an outcome that is consistent with your organisation's values. You believe that you need to challenge the team to change the approach. You need them to acknowledge the issue before coming with details.	*e.g. Your recruitment processes fail to bring in a diverse range of candidates. You want to challenge the requirement for a degree and promote alternative ways of assessing candidates.*
...confront an inconvenient truth.	You believe there is a fundamental flaw in the strategy of your business. You want to persuade senior management that a radical rethink is required. It will be necessary to make significant investment in resources, staffing, or service provisions. This will not be popular.	*e.g. Your manufacturing lines produce a well-regarded product but the market is changing. You must persuade senior leaders to invest in new manufacturing capabilities.*
...inspire them to work by core values.	You feel the team has deviated from the right path. We have been distracted by the looser values of others. We have been tempted by the easy benefits of following the status quo. You want to connect everyone to the values that we should hold closest to our hearts.	*e.g. You run a food bank. You surprise your leadership team with a talk. Obsessed with growing donations, we have lost sight of what really matters: giving dignity to the people who come.*
...create a bunker mentality.	You see your team being disrupted by expectations and criticisms from outside the group. You want the team to band together and feel this can be done by highlighting the unique values and strengths of the group. It is time to ignore outside voices, and focus on what we alone know is true.	*e.g. You open a team off-site after negative press reports on your team's activities. You want to bring everyone together to brush off the criticism and focus on the things we see as fundamental.*

 # Maverick **Task:** You are there to...

Check that you can focus on the right thing. The maverick prez-type is best when you want to...

...challenge »

You **challenge** any outmoded and obsolete thinking.
You **challenge** the established "way things are done".
You **challenge** people who fail to live by true values.

...rally »

You **rally** the audience behind pure ethics and morals.
You **rally** them to take a stand. You **rally** them to live by something great within themselves.

As you challenge your audience's beliefs and rally them behind your shared values,
you may consider one or more of the following:

question »

You question your audience: you quiz their assumptions, interrogate their beliefs, and prod their intentions. You enquire into why they ignore other possibilities. You open a doorway to consider alternative perspectives, interpretations, and opinions.

confront »

You call out the problems with the status quo. You highlight the fallacies and absurdities of present practices. You denounce beliefs and behaviours which fall short of what we should expect of ourselves. You provide a mirror to the actions of your audience, making them see the realities of their choices.

recruit »

You enlist the audience to embrace a movement, a set of ethics, a way of living. You help them remember how much they value these beliefs. You offer them a chance to be part of something independent and unique, uninhibited by authority, traditions, or societal expectations.

energise »

You awaken the inner spirit and authenticity of the audience. You remove the veil of ambivalence to trigger a fresh enthusiasm to do the right thing. You make them eager to embrace the upcoming change. You vitalise an excitement to be part of something.

Intensity of Maverick

 Mild   Medium   Hot

OUTSIDER   PROVOCATEUR   CHALLENGER   **REFORMER**   PROGRESSIVE   REBEL   **REVOLUTIONARY**

Your maverick prez-types are all there to challenge the audience and rally them together, but this can be a gentle enquiry or a clarion call for transformation.

When you want to interrogate from a safe distance, select an **outsider-maverick**. When you want to catalyse change from within, consider being a **reformer-maverick**. When you are demanding a radically new reality, and are eager to break many eggs along the way, select a **revolutionary-maverick**.

Mild-intensity **OUTSIDER** 	You are not from within their "tribe". This enables you to ask the controversial questions and make novel observations under the guise of curiosity. You can compare to your experiences with other groups who do things differently. You do this without fear of being unfaithful to the local traditions. You can (gently) challenge what they do. You can ask questions like "*Why do you...?*" and "*How come you don't...*" The audience must justify the habits and practices. Anything that actually does not make sense becomes apparent. They must, at least, reconsider their beliefs.
Medium-intensity **REFORMER** 	You are within the "tribe" but you want to drive positive change from within. You believe the group's values are strong, but that they are not being lived by. You know "we" can do better. You refuse to follow expectations of others. You show there are alternative ways of doing things. You can challenge, but with the intent to improve from within. There are things to keep the same and there are things that must be different. The audience is energised by you. They can make positive change for the tribe while keeping all that is strong with the present practices.
Hot-intensity **REVOLUTIONARY** 	Whether inside or outside the "tribe", you believe things have to be fundamentally broken down before they can be transformed and rebuilt. Making "course corrections" and "minor tweaks" will fall well short of what is needed. This will be hard, and the powerful will complain, but it is time for an uprising of reason and common sense. Your audience, once on your side, will be exhilarated to be part of something truly transformational. They will tell their grandchildren that they were there from the start.

Maverick: **Shape Sharpeners**

Tips on how to choose and arrange your content for a maverick type of presentation.

Hone Your Messaging

Make your main messages:

provocations

Set your audience a **probing challenge**. A statement that shines a light on hypocrisy or stupidity or naivety. Ideally, connect to inarguable **fundamental values and truths**.

An objection, query, protestation, call, challenge, dare, moral, virtue, value.

e.g. *"Ask not what your country can do for you – ask what you can do for your country."* John F. Kennedy.

You want your audience to be **surprised**. You want to jolt the audience out of their lazy thinking and habitual behaviours. Take what is "well known" and customary, and **shock** them so they see things completely differently.

Yet, you want to bring the audience along with you. Charge your messages with **emotional** fundamentals – the darkness of today in contrast to the brightness of an alternative tomorrow. Bridge from the negatives (e.g. frustration) to the potential positives (e.g. satisfaction) of being true to our ideals.

Shave Your Information

PRIORITISE

Things that explain what is **wrong with now** and the **values** that necessitate change.

☆ This **pain we feel** from the **status quo** and the implications of allowing it to remain.

☆ The **innate values** that we hold as fundamental – individually and collectively.

INCLUDE

✓ What is plainly wrong with the existing thinking.

✓ Dissatisfaction with the existing thinking.

✓ Fresh perspectives, options, and opinions.

✓ Unique ways of being.

✓ Content that will bind the team together behind shared ideals.

DEPRIORITISE

The **details**.

✗ Detailed data to justify your thoughts.

✗ A detailed plan.

✗ Balanced perspective of others.

✗ Details meant to appease concerns or answer questions.

Great ways to structure parts of your presentation.

Two Structure – Curate's Egg:

Arrange key content into two opposing perspectives: the flimsy benefits of the established ideas and the paired painful detriments. Set each up fully at the start and then move regularly back and forth between the two. You work to highlight how the publicised positives are insufficient against the negatives. Ideally, frame the benefits as lacking in deeper values (e.g. short-term profit) and the detriments as being more innately immoral (e.g. declining team spirit and productivity). You use this structure to show that the mass of negatives outweighs the flimsy positives.

News Structure – They Nod, You Stop!

Get to the headlines straight away – what is wrong and what you are recommending. Share the primary issue with the present situation and the value it breaks – if you get the nod, you stop! If not, move onto the next, slightly less vital, issue and broken values – if you get the nod, you stop! Repeat this, stepping to smaller issues with broken values, until the growing weight of issues pushes your audience to acknowledge things must change.

Story Structure – Pride Before a Fall:

Introduce a character who is an example of the present thinking. Seemingly, paint them in a positive light: big up minor strengths beyond what is reasonable – inch towards hyperbole. Wedge open the cracks in the thinking, bringing in inconsistencies and issues, but then excessively dismiss them. Allow absurdities to appear. Foreshadow the upcoming fall by denying the possibility of it ever happening. Finally, introduce the inevitable cliff-edge. Describe the shock and shame of the anti-hero as they crash down. They are unable to see what we all see – they were blind to what is obviously wrong in "how things are done today".

Great ways to open and close your presentation.

Include in your opening: Summarise the established thinking and the standard practices. Highlight any misguided directives coming from outside the group. As briefly as possible, articulate the reason why we must challenge all of these things. Bring in the core values that will underpin how we will think differently.

Include in your closing section: Return to the list of established thinking that you started with. Concisely and surgically reinforce how our fundamental values mean we must challenge each and every one.

 # Maverick: **Shift Keys**

Signal

Indicate to your audience how to listen.

Show immediately that you are looking at things from a different perspective. Do something different to the standard way things are done: dress differently, talk differently, run the presentation somewhere different.

Warn your audience that you will challenge existing "ways things are done". Early on, reference the irrefutable values that will underpin why we must change our thinking.

 ## Spoken Language

Your language is distinct. It sets you apart from the norms of your scenario.

You can be changeable: at times provocative as you challenge, at times cool and calm as you probe, and at other times openly passionate.

Language should clearly divide yourself (and your audience) from the stuffy "establishment". If they are overly optimistic, then you are pessimistic. If they are overly data driven, you will focus on real stories.

Keep to simple explanations and standard phrases. Leave overly ornate dialogue to others.

You are comfortable talking of values and ethics, or right and wrong.

Emotional language:

O Show confusion, **anger**, frustration, and **disgust**. Things are not as they should be.

O Be steadfast and **aspirational** when talking of the fundamental values we must live by.

 ## Body Language

Your postures should be strong yet relaxed. Mavericks can be nonchalant and composed – unruffled by outside concerns. You are completely comfortable with eye contact.

You are more likely to stand uncentred: leaning on one hip, head angled. You likely stand at an angle to your audience (not square on).

Your gestures may be fairly small – you do not need to enlarge yourself for others. The exception can be when you are making your most impassioned points.

You may sit on a table edge. You may lean against a wall. You may stand with hands in your pockets.

Your clothing is likely to be distinct and unique, reflecting your individuality. You do not feel the need to conform to any uniform or passing fashion.

Beware: your audience will note what you do before and after your presentation. Maintain your individuality and confidence in your message.

Staging

Stage the space in a way that goes against traditions. If people normally stand behind a lectern, you roam free. If everyone dances around the stage, you calmly lean on the lectern.

Find unusual ways to use the space. Avoid "centre stage". Sit in the audience, lean on a table, ignore the plush chair that is set centrally and drag one into the space from the side.

Define zones in the space that represent: 1) the things and ideas that you are challenging; 2) the things that should be based on our values. Move to the zone that matches your focus at that point.

Virtual: Avoid virtual or blurred backgrounds. Find an unusual position with a distinct backdrop.

Small room: Make the room feel different. Maybe arrange so you can use opposite sides of the room.

Large room: Look to break from routines – an extreme they won't expect e.g. reject all the technology and lighting available and just talk to them.

Visuals

Look to break the established rules: dismiss the standard company template! Or if using a corporate deck, find ways to graffiti it with your own individual observations and thoughts.

Step away from very well-prepared slide-decks. Rely more on simple slides and other visuals. Consider the use of colour to emphasise the difference between the status quo and the proposed solution.

Rely more on simple statements than detailed prose.

Keep diagrams and charts as simplified or focussed purely on the major points. Look to include quotes and images from real people living real lives.

You are more likely to move away from PowerPoint completely: grab a flip chart and draw a single message; bring in an object that exemplifies an issue; put up a large poster with the key figure that emphasises our failures; or just stand and talk, relying on your body language.

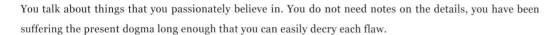

How To Manage Your Presenter Notes

You talk about things that you passionately believe in. You do not need notes on the details, you have been suffering the present dogma long enough that you can easily decry each flaw.

You may have some simple notes. A few words typed on your smartphone on the values we choose to live by.
A few bullets on an index card to remind you of the main stories you plan to share. If you are quoting specific rules, before slamming them for their absurdity, you may read these aloud from the governance website.

Interact

You want to engage in dialogue with your audience. You want to push them to think critically, to challenge them, and to get them to consider new possibilities. However, you do not want to give them total freedom – you want to keep away from exact plans and energy-sapping details.

Freedom to give your audience

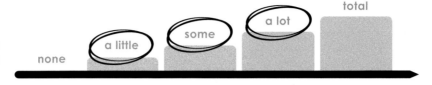

Fundamentally, you want to create a thought-provoking atmosphere in which they can consider how their values should make them rethink their present beliefs and actions.

Therefore:

O Question and challenge your audience.

O Encourage radical thinking – encourage others to break constraints.

O Encourage them to envision new versions of today – new ways of being.

How? *Example processes include:*

O Ask rhetorical, direct and provocative questions to the audience – *"What if everything we have been told about this is wrong?"*; *"Who thinks we can stay as we are?"*

O Ask questions that encourage them to vocalise dissatisfaction with the present thinking – *"How do you really feel about these arcane rules?"*

O Challenge them to connect present behaviours with core values – *"How does this plan get us closer to being the company we choose to be?"*

Ready Yourself

☐ Grab a piece of paper and note down:
   O What annoys you with the established thinking?
   O Why must we change?
   O What are the values we hold that compel us to change?

☐ Before the presentation, look to keep some distance from people. Consciously disconnect from people who epitomise things you will soon challenge.

☐ Do a good selection of stretches, especially of your arms and legs. You want to release as much tension as you can.

☐ Complete a personal visualisation. Find a quiet space away from the room, get comfortable, and visualise yourself walking confidently into the performance space. See yourself talking confidently and calmly.

☐ Remind yourself that nothing matters more than your message. No tech failures or surprise interruptions will knock you off your game.

Maverick Prez-type **Watch Outs!**

Beware the dark side of the maverick prez-type. Avoid:

Mindless Arsonist	Emotionally Unengaged
It is counterproductive to demand that everything be burnt down. Acknowledge that some things should stay as they are, even as you focus on what must change.	Convey some emotional intelligence. Avoid being so set on the changes needed that you don't show you have considered the impact on the people involved.

Handling likely objections: You will start with the pain of the present situation, but remember to get full buy-in to the values that will underpin what comes in its place. You need to bring people with you. The larger the transformation, the more you need to show the connection to true values that they share.

Maverick Prez-type **Powerful Pairings**

Start as the **maverick** prez-type to shake up the audience's thinking (things must change) and bring togetherness (we are the ones to do this). Then jump to the **creator** prez-type to explain the detailed plan.

As the **maverick** prez-type, challenge the present thinking and push for why a change is needed. Then hop to the **magician** prez-type to introduce the vision/tech/initiative that will power the transition.

Start as **jester** prez-type, entertaining your audience. Start to probe and highlight absurdities in the situation. Hop to **maverick** prez-type to turn these probes into provocations – something must change!

Tricky Transitions: Moving between **maverick** prez-type and **ruler** prez-type or **sage** prez-type can undermine the spirit of transformation that you are inspiring. You want your audience to break free from the shackles of authority (**ruler**) and from the dogma of established wisdom (**sage**).

Jester

Jester

fool

player

wit

funster

entertainer

raconteur

merrymaker

As a jester-type presenter you encourage the audience to **release their tensions**. Through playfulness and spontaneity you help the audience **smile more and worry less**.

The audience benefits as you **enable them to connect with each other** through shared laughter, shared fun, and shared games. You may highlight the folly of existing thinking (the dogma).

But **mostly you play**.

The **Essence** of the Jester

From Fiction: Wipe away your image of a man in a multicoloured outfit and bell-laden hat; jesters appear in many forms in fiction. Consider Fred and George Weasley from the Harry Potter stories. They are irreverent in most situations, playing practical jokes and owning a joke shop. They are the comic relief; they bring a lightening smile whether in the lightest times or the darkest times.

Cartoon characters like Bugs Bunny are full of chaos and joy, always mocking those who deserve to be mocked. We, the audience, love the anarchy and the fun because the target of the jibe deserves to be jested.

Remember Rocket Racoon, from the Marvel *Guardians of the Galaxy*; he is the first to highlight the absurdity of any situation. Similarly, Donkey from *Shrek*, R2-D2 from *Star Wars*, Olaf from *Frozen*, and Timon and Pumbaa from *The Lion King*. These are all fictional characters encouraging others to relax, enjoy today, and leave other concerns to tomorrow.

From Real World: Awards evenings are often highly charged events (with more losers than winners). So most, like the Oscars or the Tonys, are hosted by a comedic performer. Their role is to puncture the air of tension and allow people to relax and enjoy themselves.

Sometimes the topic itself brings tension. Find "I got 99 problems... palsy is just one" by Maysoon Zayid on TED.com;[29] you will experience a glorious example of a real person brilliantly embodying their jester-style delivery to bring us into her world and her reality.

> *"Laughter not only lightens the load, but it can also give you a sense of perspective."*
> Fama Francisco:
> P&G CEO of Global Baby, Feminine & Family Care

Being your jester prez-type helps your audience **come together** and feel together. You allow them to pause from any tensions or concerns and **focus on having fun**. You create an atmosphere and activities that encourage people to **share experiences**. The serious can wait – for this moment we play.

The Versatile Presenter

Jester: **When to Select**

Choose to be a jester prez-type when you want everyone to relax, sweep away excessive seriousness, and to encourage trust to form (or be strengthened) through the audience.

Select the jester prez-type when you want to...

...build team spirit and togetherness.	You want to help the audience to connect and enjoy each other's company. Your primary objective is to build trust across the group; to enable harmony and productive future collaboration or just to help make this a fun place to work.	*e.g. You are opening a team off-site to bring the whole team together for the first time. You want stalwarts and newbies to build connections.*
...strengthen a client relationship.	You are there to develop your working relationship with a client or internal stakeholder. So let them see that you are relaxed and comfortable in their company. By being playful, you encourage them to see you as someone they want to work with because you are fun, open and honest.	*e.g. You are presenting to an important client who you know, but with whom you have not yet built rapport.*
...relax a concerned audience.	You need to soothe and settle an anxious audience. People are worried about a serious topic. They may be struggling to see beyond the implications for them personally. You encourage people to dismiss fears and preconceptions. This will move an audience towards being able to listen and engage in the information.	*e.g. You are opening a meeting to agree the response to a new competitive market entry. Rumours are flying around. Many people are concerned about the impact on the business (and their employment).*
...encourage a dialogue where disagreements lie.	You create, through a playful air, a safe environment for people to express and discuss disagreements. Nothing will change (yet), but you create an atmosphere where people can smile together, sowing the seeds for future compromise and change.	*e.g. You are summarising two competing strategies for how to invest in the business. You need both sides to step outside their entrenched positions.*

Jester **Task:** You are there to...

Check that you can focus on the right thing. The jester prez-type is best when you want to...

...entertain »

You **entertain** the audience with activities and games. You **entertain** them with quips and jibes. You **entertain** them with anecdotes and stories.

...connect »

You **connect** the audience together through shared joy. You **connect** them through shared experiences. You **connect** them through audience participation.

As you lighten the mood and connect people, concentrate on one or more of the following:

play »

You embody a sense of playfulness. You embrace opportunities to be spontaneous in the moment. You enable others to play: through games and group performances. You form simple but silly "rules" to follow. You encourage volunteers or everyone to get involved.

lighten »

You encourage a more easy-going atmosphere. You downplay seriousness. You focus on activities that hold their attention and are enjoyable. You soften tensions and quieten concerns. You skilfully find the light side of even serious topics.

ease »

You find ways to make things feel simple and manageable. You strip away complexities. You encourage them to place concerns and anxieties to one side (for now). Hold their attention on the here and now, and the joy to be found in simple things.

amuse »

You look for things that will bring a smile. If something seems laughable, you laugh at it. If something seems ridiculous, you ridicule it. You will stay within the boundaries of what is acceptable to this audience and environment, while being free to laugh and have fun.

# **Intensity** of Jester

 Mild   Medium   Hot

FOOL   PLAYER   WIT   **FUNSTER**   ENTERTAINER   RACONTEUR   **MERRYMAKER**

As a jester you may plan to be funny yourself, or you may choose to lead activities that let the audience be funny.

When you want to keep all potential mockery aimed at you, select a **fool-jester**. When you want everyone involved in the fun, aim right into the middle of this prez-type and select a **funster-jester**. When the need is to lead everyone into accepting the silly and ridiculous, and you have the confidence to do so, switch on your full **merrymaker-jester**.

Mild-intensity **FOOL** 	You will make mistakes, muddle and blunder. You will amplify your lack of knowledge and skill. The audience quickly realises this is an act and not to be taken seriously. You may stumble on truths, but if you do it will be through chance. You will be full of joy, and quick to find the fun in things. You will smile at your pratfalls. You make everyone else feel good by the clownish things that you do. You highlight how much more they know. You also bring to attention stupid questions and dumb perspectives. These can be invaluable as no one else will worry about asking their "dumb" questions.
Medium-intensity **FUNSTER** 	The audience relies on you to find the fun. In any situation, there is a lighter side for you to bring forward. You grab all opportunities to bring enjoyment to the situation. You encourage everyone else to relax and to join in. If there are serious things to consider, you will not belittle them, but you may encourage people to hold that thought for later. For now, let us smile and look for the positives. The audience will depend on you to "turn a frown upside-down". You will start games, encourage interaction, and defuse tensions.
Hot-intensity **MERRYMAKER**	You will be the "queen"/"king" of fun. Everyone waits in anticipation, knowing that you guarantee a good time. You encourage everyone to fully embrace the fun that freedom brings. You do not just encourage the fun, you lead everyone towards it. You may be the games master, leading people through the most playful experiences. You may be the master comic, expertly stitching together anecdote after anecdote.

3 SHARPEN YOUR PREZ CONTENT

 Jester: **Shape Sharpeners**

Tips on how to choose and arrange your content for a jester type of presentation.

Hone Your Messaging

Make your main messages:

witticisms

It does not have to be hilarious, but it is best if your main message is funny or reminds them of something funny. Something that, in some way, brings a collective smile.

A joke, a quip, a witty rhyme, an absurd observation, a smart callback, a gentle jest.

e.g. *"We pluck the lemons, you get the plums."* 1960 ad for Volkswagen Beetle – Julian Koenig.

Find a quirky and **surprising** turn of phrase. An angle or perspective that the audience won't expect but will instantly enjoy. Or, find a surprising way of delivering the line, e.g.: sung, silly accent, adding a fun gesture, etc.

Look for **repetition**. Create messages with rhyme and rhythm, with cadence, or alliteration. Transform a message from *"We will meet every Monday to review Project Merlin"* to something like *"Merlin matters, so we mingle every Monday"*

Shave Your Information

PRIORITISE

Imaginative ideas, **repeated** in varied and creative ways.

☆ **Whatever is funniest** (silliest, more ridiculous, most satirical, etc.) and unimportant.

☆ **Content that can be gamified.** Especially if through repeating processes e.g. call and response.

INCLUDE

✓ Funny anecdotes, that the whole audience will enjoy.

✓ Poems, songs, rhyming language.

✓ Anything looking from an unusual perspective.

✓ Cartoons, funny photos.

✓ Content that can be represented with fun props/objects.

DEPRIORITISE

The **serious**.

✗ Sensitive or contentious topics (collectively or individually).

✗ Detailed analysis (unless it is funny).

✗ Critical elements of strategies and plans.

Great ways to structure parts of your presentation.

Story Structure – Anecdote:

This can be any story involving comedy scrapes, pratfalls, etc. These are best when the embarrassment you describe is endured by you (or someone everyone knows will be happy to be the butt of the joke). You may follow a classic triumphant fool story:

1) Everyday Fool: a foolish person, ill-equipped for the world they live in, is laughed at.

2) But Seriously: something happens that forces the fool to leave their carefree existence and engage in real challenges.

3) Pratfalls: obstacles that the fool struggles to overcome, but through luck and honesty they succeed.

4) Carefree Wins the Day: a final ordeal where the fool's naivety and carefree essence is integral to their success.

Two Structure – Serious and Silly:

Laughter often comes from comparisons. This may be a double act (straight man and comic). Or from contrasting the serious with the silly. Options include:

O An expert serious view in combination with an irreverent novice view.

O A serious goal (e.g. final sales targets) paired with a frivolous goal (e.g. funniest photo of product in store).

O How we imagine the initiative will look in-store contrasted with the likely reality.

Three Structure – Joke Triple:

A classic joke can be built in three parts (sometimes called a "triple"). Part one suggests an idea; part two infers a pattern; part three breaks the pattern (thus creating the laugh). You may not be looking to create a fully belly laugh, but following this pattern will create a funny moment.

Great ways to open and close your presentation.

Include in your opening: Something you know will relax everyone and make them smile. Maybe a short story that you know will generate laughter. Include content or a process that will get the audience interacting early.

Include in your closing section: Summarise the fun that has been had, focussing on the brilliantly joyous responses from the audience themselves. Highlight your funniest main message. Maybe end on a final callback – an idea stated before but now with a final twist.

 Jester: **Shift Keys**

Signal

Indicate to your audience how to listen.

You should find a way to show your audience that you are going to be playful and jocular (to avoid them becoming confused or offended). This can be as simple as telling them (*"let's take a few minutes to get playful with these ideas"*). You can start with a light-hearted joke or witty observation or an obvious exaggeration (*"When I started working on this project 2,000 years ago…"*).

Adding visual cues can help everyone know not to take things too seriously (or literally), e.g. a silly hat or a full comedy costume.

 ## Spoken Language

Enthusiastically use language that is playful, irreverent, etc. Revel in quirky phrases. Language can be provocative, perhaps crude, even sweary (as long as it is socially appropriate and respectful).

Be self-effacing: aim the most biting words at yourself.

Express ideas simply, even deliberately simplistically. Absurdities, hyperbole, exaggerations, non-truths.

Embrace accents and voices other than your normal one. Laugh yourself – it is contagious. Laugh at the ideas you share.

Emotional language:

○ Be full of **anticipation** for the fun we will have.

○ Ooze **curiosity** in what will happen.

○ Find **joy** and laughter in as much as you can.

 ## Body Language

Aim body language towards your audience, always attentive to their responses. You will direct them to the funny elements of your content, but always be ready to step back towards your audience.

Gestures will likely be fluid and broad. You may exaggerate your movements.

Smile often.

Keep on the balls of your feet with your knees bent (as Jacque Tati said, *"comedy begins in the legs"*).

Use clothes and accessories as a way to signal it is time for fun.

It could be something clearly incongruous to the situation (e.g. a dinner jacket at a weekly team meeting), or a costume (e.g. mascot outfit), or just an outlandish shirt.

Staging

Set the space out in a fun way. Create a "stage" area, with enough space for you to move around (or dance) as you want (and for volunteers to join you).

Feel free to move anywhere and everywhere. Look for surprising areas to move to (e.g. standing on a table). That said, you definitely know where centre stage is, where you engage and entertain the entire room.

Create a safe space for them to relax in (free to play) e.g. everyone can see the "stage" area; shut blinds if windows mean they can be overlooked; make it obvious how they can exit the area. It is hard to relax and play when you feel trapped.

Virtual: Get creative with what they can see through your webcam, e.g. virtual background, odd location. Play with virtual views (e.g. 3D room, together mode).

Small room: Shift furniture to create a playful space, e.g. quiz set-up, stage and audience, comedy club.

Large room: Use music and lighting to signal fun! Find ways to bring people from the audience into the "stage" area through games and interactions.

Visuals

If using slides, prioritise funny photos, cartoons, silly images, etc. This is not the time for a long, detailed slide deck.

You are keen to break formal conventions – find ways to provoke and surprise. Bring in other types of visuals: props, posters, surprising objects, etc.

Use yourself as a "visual tool" e.g. act out elements of a story; embody in physical form the metaphorical idea that you share.

Consider making any visual bigger, brighter, more colourful, sillier. Get creative.

Keep to "low design" (rather than "high design"). The imperfect is normally funnier.

The one area to design more carefully (and with key details) are instructions associated with any games to be played e.g. quizzes, activities, team games, etc.

How To Manage Your Presenter Notes

Ideally present from minimal notes. Maybe a single mind map, or a few pointers on an index card. You want to be free to be spontaneous in the moment, open to adapt to whatever happens in the room. Where you need to speak accurately, maybe to deliver a funny story, practise it enough to be off script.

Interact

You want the audience involved. Maybe simply laugh together, maybe to interact eagerly, maybe to participate in a range of frivolous games. You want them to connect to the fun you are having, and the joy that comes directly by sharing the fun together.

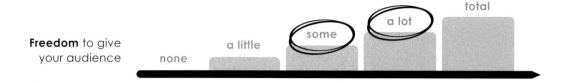

Freedom to give your audience

none — a little — some — a lot — total

You want to create the sense of freedom while holding some level of control. You do not want chaos; you want freedom within conscious boundaries. Any game needs some rules.

Therefore:

O   Create clear "rules of the game" – so everyone can play freely with certainty.

O   Look for carefree competition – games of tomfoolery, with chance more vital than skill, leading to silly prizes.

O   Find creative ways to get people involved, whether that is the whole audience or participating "volunteers".

How? *Example processes include:*

O   Silly games with volunteers – *"We have two teams up on stage ready to go – let's jump straight into the first game..."*

O   Fun dialogue with individuals in the audience [said with a smile] – *"Ralph, you look like you think you could do better – what should we have done?"*

O   Call and response with the audience – *"Our launch of BEARDY will only work if we enable men with poorer beards to confidently grow one. So, we must remember that 'Each hairless chin is a potential win'. With me, 'Each hairless chin...'" [leading response from audience] "'...is a potential win'".*

Ready Yourself

☐   Do not over-rehearse. Practise key stories and funny moments, but keep yourself free to adapt your flow and your language. Mistakes you make will turn into opportunities for more laughter.

☐   Do a full body warm-up. You want to be free and fluid in your movements. Ensure you stretch out your arms and legs.

Jester Prez-type **Watch Outs!**

Beware the dark side of the jester prez-type. Avoid:

Flippancy

You are there to bring joy and fun in the moment, but be careful not to undermine the importance of the topic under discussion.

Forced Fun

Not every moment is one where an audience will appreciate finding fun together. Sometimes they want to be allowed to just sit and listen.

Handling likely objections: It needs to be the right time and place for levity and play. You may need to reassure them that we will not forget or undermine seriousness. We are merely choosing to step away from it for a while.

Jester Prez-type **Powerful Pairings**

Set your credibility high by embodying the **sage** prez-type to work through the knowledge and insights. Then jump briefly into the **jester** prez-type to increase your likeability, perhaps sharing fun facts or humorous observations, before returning to the **sage** prez-type.

You predominantly embody the **student** prez-type, carefully setting the credibility of experts that you have learnt from. Periodically you step into the **jester** prez-type to entertain and engage your audience.

Start as the **maverick** prez-type to create a sense of being part of an exciting new change, one that better fits our values. But there will be nervousness with breaking away from existing norms. Move to the **jester** prez-type to relax people. Bring levity, play a game, get a smile.

Tricky Transitions: Moving between **jester** prez-type and **ruler** prez-type or **explorer** prez-type can jar for the audience. They want to relax, which will feel challenging if suddenly asked to go to new places (**explorer**) or to absorb very clear directions (**ruler**).

Lover

Lover

advocate

buddy

sidekick

cheerleader

endorser

admirer

#1 fan

As a lover-type presenter you make everyone in the audience **feel great** about themselves and their team. You **celebrate their successes**. Your audience savours the **praise** and **acclamation** that you lavish on them. This builds their self-esteem and confidence in the team they are part of.

The audience **appreciates** the gifts you offer them. If there is something they deserve or desire, you are first to provide it for them. You remind them that they are **great as they are** (so keep doing what you are doing).

The Essence of the Lover

From Fiction: In many stories there is a sidekick or best friend who encourages the hero forward through unwavering support. Think Ron Weasley for Harry Potter, Samwise Gamgee for Frodo Baggins, Toto for Dorothy, Chewbacca for Han Solo, Charlotte for Elizabeth Bennet, the whole sorority for Elle Woods (*Legally Blonde*). When the hero needs a fillip, a reminder on their abilities and their worth, the sidekick is there.

In other stories, the lover is more of an inspiring mentor figure. In the film *Dead Poets Society*, Robin Williams' character, John Keating, starts as a maverick, compelling his students to see their education through new eyes. However, for much of the film he is a supporting mentor; he propels his students to look inside to value their own passions and motivations, to trust their own interests and desires (and to "seize the day").

From Real World: In the real world, we look to individuals who publicly recognise excellent achievements and take action to inspire others. In her shows and in her writing, Oprah Winfrey encourages self-discovery and self-improvement and acknowledges and provides a platform to those whose achievements can inspire others.

Princess Diana's funeral was held in London in 1997. Her brother, Earl Spencer, delivered a moving tribute.[30] It was controversial at the time (it directly challenged the actions of the monarchy), but at its heart it is a eulogy full of loving praise, painting a picture of a sister who was talented, hard-working, and brave, yet someone who was vulnerable. He compels us to see her as someone who deserves the greatest of admiration from us all.

Being your lover prez-type **makes your audience feel good**. You **celebrate** their successes. **Praise** and **applaud** their finest qualities (and dismiss the relevance of any weaknesses). By recognising and appreciating their contributions you make your audience **feel valuable and valued**.

 # Lover: **When to Select**

Choose to be a lover prez-type when you need to make your audience feel valuable and valued, building confidence in themselves and each other.

Select the lover prez-type when you want to...

...show appreciation for a particular individual or team.	You recognise that an individual or team has gone above and beyond their expected scope of work to deliver a successful outcome. You want them to feel acknowledged and appreciated.	*e.g. You bring the team together to review recent successes, announcing that they are nominated for an industry award.*
...recognise behaviours that you want to see continued.	You want to encourage people in the organisation to embody key behaviours. One team has been an exemplar in their recent conduct. You want to make this team feel great about this so they continue working in this way, and you want to encourage others to follow their attitude and approach.	*e.g. Beardy Team has completed a potentially fractious negotiation while staying respectful and professional. You want to publicly endorse this behaviour. You present their work as a case study at the yearly off-site.*
...build the confidence of an individual.	You have identified a talented individual with great potential but who lacks confidence. You note areas they are strong in and acknowledge those, building their confidence to develop their skills and abilities further.	*e.g. You deliver the introduction speech for Jo at an internal awards ceremony. You take extra time to celebrate Jo's great work.*
...build confidence within a team that they have the skills to be successful.	Your team is facing a challenging situation and you are aware they are not collaborating as effectively as they could be. You emphasise the expertise within the team asserting that, if they work collaboratively, they have all the talents and abilities to deliver amazing results.	*e.g. At a team off-site, you make a twenty-minute presentation where you passionately talk about the team's strengths (individual and collective).*

Lover **Task:** You are there to...

Check that you can focus on the right thing. The lover prez-type is best when you want to...

...appreciate »

You **appreciate** their attitude – the efforts involved.
You **appreciate** their talents – the skills that they bring.
You **appreciate** their successes, big and small.

...acclaim »

You **acclaim** their best qualities. You **acclaim** each success from the sidelines. You **acclaim** achievements (past and present) to key stakeholders.

As you appreciate and acclaim your audience, and build their confidence in themselves and each other, concentrate on one or more of the following:

value »

You recognise the behaviours and results that the individual or team has demonstrated. You will communicate the specific details in the unique things that they bring, and highlight the great benefits that these bring to us all.

praise »

You express warm approval and admiration of the individual or team. You compliment their achievements – what they have done. You also praise how they went about it – calling out how their best features were core to their well-deserved results.

encourage »

You remind them of how great they are. You celebrate past successes and cheer every recent accomplishment. This pushes them to believe fully in themselves – they already have what it takes to flourish. You provide the fillip – a burst of confidence in their abilities and talents.

reward »

You give them gifts (as they justly deserve). These will be more than mere tokens. They may be small treats – minor indulgences that remind them they are appreciated. They may be major treasures – significant awards to remind them they are uniquely acclaimed.

Intensity of Lover

Mild	Medium	Hot

ADVOCATE   BUDDY   SIDEKICK   **CHEERLEADER**   ENDORSER   ADMIRER   **#1 FAN**

As a lover prez-type you are fully focussed on the wishes and desires of your audience, but your level of appreciation can vary.

When you are highlighting their strengths, select an **advocate-lover**. When you are endorsing them for all that they do, select a **cheerleader-lover**. When you are showing unwavering admiration for all aspects of who they are, select a **#1 fan-lover**.

Mild-intensity

ADVOCATE

You are a vocal supporter, publicly and privately. You can acknowledge slight weaknesses, keeping your positive praise realistic, but are fast to highlight their achievements. You are optimistic about what they will achieve in the future.

Your audience feels that you see the good in them. This brings confidence and an eagerness to do well.

Medium-intensity

CHEERLEADER

You hugely value what they have achieved and want to champion them with everyone who will listen. You find public ways to recognise their behaviour and achievements. While you might be aware of issues along the way, you focus only on their successes.

Your audience feels buoyed by your words and actions. It encourages them to see the very best in themselves. They feel energised.

Hot-intensity

#1 FAN

You are completely besotted by their qualities: they are the most impressive, the most deserving, and the most accomplished. You don't mind who knows it; your adoration is complete. In your opinion, everything they have done is wonderful. You are euphoric. Any issues or problems are entirely immaterial (and likely the fault of bad luck or cheating by others).

Your audience feels thrilled as you describe the very best of their talents and abilities. You fill them with unrivalled confidence in themselves.

 Lover: **Shape Sharpeners**

Tips on how to choose and arrange your content for a lover type of presentation.

Hone Your Messaging

Make your main messages:

plaudits

You lead with an expression of praise or approval that recognises an individual or team's talents, behaviours, or achievements.

An accolade, compliment, tribute, homage, celebration, gift.

e.g. *"Your results this quarter have been outstanding. Please join me in a round of applause for the whole team."*

Use **emotive** words that celebrate the audience's abundant talents and achievements. They are not just "good", they are "great" and probably "the greatest".

Ensure you share your message, of admiration or appreciation **repeatedly**. Announcing their greatness once is never going to be enough – the cheerleader keeps cheering.

Shave Your Information

PRIORITISE

Their greatest successes and **their greatest qualities.**

☆ **Evidence of success:** past achievements, present glories, future wins.

☆ **Positive qualities** of the audience, looked at from many angles and perspectives.

INCLUDE

✓ Example stories that bring to life the behaviour and aspects that you admire.

✓ Accolades from the respected sources (e.g. key leaders).

✓ Evidence of how any competitors are inferior.

✓ Experiential and multi-sensory content (e.g. videos, impressive demos).

✓ Secrets you only share with them.

DEPRIORITISE

The **unflattering.**

✗ Things that are basic expectations of that role or team.

✗ Suggestions for improvement.

✗ Successes of anyone outside the group.

✗ Suggestions they change.

✗ Talk of their failings.

Great ways to
structure parts of
your presentation.

One Structure – Greatest Highlight:

An umbrella thought, possibly of celebration or recognition, is the focus of your presentation. You devote the whole presentation to a single quality of theirs: a talent, their recent business success, a value they live by, etc.

For example: You bring every section of your talk to a celebration of the team's record-breaking annual business results; you connect every element of your talk to their pioneering work in online marketing; you reference every member to highlight a story of their impressive persistence.

Story Structure – At Their Best:

Tell the full story of a past success of theirs. Describe the challenges that they overcame, highlighting how their finest qualities were integral to their success. Reference the admiration in them expressed by others.

News Structure – Highlights Reel:

Take content that explains all of the audience's fantastic qualities, then sequence from greatest, to great, to very good. You start with the greatest compliment and work through all of the content in decreasing significance. When the audience has heard enough, they can ask you to stop (or move onto the next section), having heard your thoughts on their greatest qualities. Or if they are enjoying the praise, they will appreciate how you are able to name so many of their positive qualities, even down to seemingly minor attributes.

Great ways to
open and close
your presentation.

Include in your opening: Start by praising them unconditionally. Promise celebration. Tell the audience how the examples you will be sharing were chosen e.g. by a popular vote, based on results, or your own opinion. Share your sense of pride in the team and their achievements.

Include in your closing section: Recap the impressiveness of the achievements celebrated here. Reinforce your commitment to, and confidence in, the team. Be appreciative, positive and celebratory. Ideally end with a final gift (e.g. a chocolate, a drink in the bar after work, confirmation of project investment, etc.).

Lover: **Shift Keys**

Signal

Indicate to your audience how to listen.

Praise them – make it clear that you are here to remind them of their many great qualities. Show how much you appreciate the opportunity to be with them. Promise and give gifts. Be clear that you will give them all the time that they need, to provide all that they may want.

If you have an endearing nickname or moniker for them, use it.

Spoken Language

Use positive language that communicates your appreciation of them. Allow your praising synonyms to run wild e.g. fabulous, wonderful, excellent, impressive, outstanding...

The appreciation you want to convey is for the team, or individuals within a team, so predominantly the use of 'you' (not 'we') is appropriate.

Highlight when you are sharing confidences and secrets.

Talk of what they deserve (in comparison to what they need).

Emotional language:

O Talk with **admiration** of the team, or individuals within the team.

O Add a sense of **anticipation** for the great things they will do in the near future.

O Share your joy in spending time with them.

Body Language

Keep stance and gestures open but not too big – you want to avoid seeming overpowering or overly prominent (they are what is important). You will mostly face your audience (point your feet towards them), arms reaching towards the people you are praising. Regularly raise your palms upwards, and you may find you gently lower your chin (in a very minor bow).

You will smile, enjoying that you are the one to highlight their strengths and talents.

Stay attentive to your audience, make eye contact with as many of the team as possible, and definitely those whose achievements you are celebrating. You may mirror the body language of the audience at times.

You are likely to dress up a little for the celebration, as you wish to impress them (but you will avoid looking significantly smarter than them).

Staging

The whole space should feel special (e.g. balloons?) and focussed on their wishes. Can you provide tasty drinks and snacks?

You want to stay close to your audience, so gravitate towards them. If audience members come onto the stage, you step back and insist they take centre stage.

Arrange seating (and lighting) so the audience is highlighted. Seating should be as comfortable as you can make it (an extra cushion?).

Be in the space ready to greet them warmly when they arrive. Stay in the room until they leave.

Virtual: Make an extra effort to make your webcam and room background look attractive, but prioritise their webcams over yours on the platform.

Small room: Set up so they get the best seats, the best view of the slides (and window view). Ensure you take the least comfortable chair (or take no chair at all).

Large room: Work with the venue to make the lighting warm, appealing and aimed at the audience. Create a special place on stage for when you bring up people from the audience.

Visuals

The visuals should reflect the team and their accomplishments. Photographs of the team should be large and clearly visible. Data charts should focus on, and vividly spotlight, their record results. Videos should be upbeat, engaging and enthusiastic. Minimise details that will be uninteresting to the audience.

All visuals should be well designed and formed in a way that will please the audience. Go the extra mile on aesthetics and design. Find ways to add sounds, music, elements they will enjoy interacting with directly.

Can elements be turned into gifts or prizes? An award, a celebration cake, etc.

Double-check for spelling mistakes and data inaccuracies – make sure it looks like you spent time to ensure everything is as it should be.

All key materials will be easily available to the audience during and after the talk. Share handouts (digital or analogue) during or straight after the presentation.

How To Manage Your Presenter Notes

Your enthusiasm and appreciation of their finest qualities must come across as genuinely heartfelt. We know what we love about people without the need for scripted notes. However, it is different when you detail their achievements and tributes from others. Then they will appreciate your completeness and accuracy so you read these directly from your notes. Similarly, when you are praising individuals in the audience, have a list ready on your iPad to ensure no one is missed.

Interact

You feel beholden to this audience and treasure their input. You are eager to halt your presentation at any moment the audience chooses to speak, so you can listen to their thoughts and wishes. You are eager to tailor your presentation to their interests throughout.

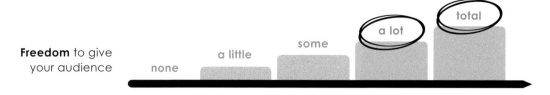

Ultimately, though, you have a message, so you may need to nudge their choices.

Therefore:

O Plan ways to regularly check that the audience is getting from you what they want. This is often as simple as asking them.

O Seek ways to gain their thoughts and perspectives – in this moment their opinions hold the most weight.

O Design interactions which give them significant control. Give them free rein to ask you whatever they want, in as much detail as they want.

O Look for activities that will be experiential and pleasurable for them.

How? *Example processes include:*

O Encouraging a demonstration of appreciation for each other – *"Please join me in a round of applause for the whole team."*

O Open questions to them on content flow – *"What would you like me to cover next?"*

O Offering them opportunities to add perspectives – *"I would love to hear your perspective – is there anything that you would like to add?"*

Ready Yourself

☐ Grab a piece of paper and note down answers to questions like: What do you appreciate most about this audience? What are some of their greatest achievements? What will they value most from you? What can you give them?

☐ Be sure you know the names of the people you are praising. For example, if giving out awards, who is winning and what they did to deserve it.

☐ Do a full technical rehearsal and dress rehearsal. You want to know how everything will work; you want to look prepared and polished. If giving gifts, where are they and how will they be handed out?

☐ Invest the time to do a full warm-up. They deserve you looking and sounding your best. You will want to convey energy and excitement.

Lover Prez-type **Watch Outs!**

Beware the dark side of the lover prez-type. Avoid:

Blind Adoration

Beware of having such a strong positive bias towards an individual or team that their contributions are not objectively assessed.

Undermining Your Own Worth

Be careful not to put so much energy into building up the team that, eventually the value that you bring is brought into question.

Handling likely objections: Ongoing, you can only support the team if you are also recognised as being valued and valuable. Be careful to ensure you don't undermine yourself, to the team or your managers/sponsors, by only publicising the achievements of the team without recognising your role in their success.

Lover Prez-type **Powerful Pairings**

Start as the **sage** prez-type to teach the knowledge that the audience needs to know. Then jump to the **lover** prez-type, making the audience confident in their ability to use the knowledge. Help them feel that the knowledge is desirable, almost a gift to those with the talents to use it (i.e. them).

Start as the **lover** prez-type, highlighting and heralding their great features and successes. Such appreciation can feel intense, so hop in and out of the **jester** prez-type to break the tension.

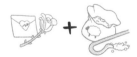

Start as the **lover** prez-type, establish how you value and appreciate them. Then skip over to the **caregiver** prez-type to offer guidance and support in the amazing work they do.

Tricky Transitions: Moving between **lover** prez-type and **hero** prez-type or **creator** prez-type may break the bond of trust with the audience. They need to feel your focussed devotion in them, so you cannot ask them to risk their skin for a higher cause (**hero**) and you cannot also be enraptured by your great design (**creator**).

Everyman

Everyman

newbie

equal

colleague

ally

friend

kin

compatriot

As an everyman-type presenter you **unite the audience behind their shared history and aligned purpose**. You **emphasise how they rely on each other**. You focus on the group's identity and what they have succeeded in achieving together.

You want them to see each other as equals and to **collaborate for mutual success**. You want people to **trust and support each other**.

The Essence of the Everyman

> *"All humanity is one undivided and indivisible family."*
> Mahatma Gandhi

From Fiction: In most stories, the hero character actually starts as an ordinary everyday person. You see them doing normal things, going through a normal day or normal experiences any of us can relate to.

Harry Potter is first shown as an eleven-year-old, living in suburbia, about to go to secondary school. Miles Morales (Spider-Man), a teenager trying to pass college exams. Mulan, a young woman going through the traditional rituals of her Chinese village. Miss Marple, an old lady visiting a family friend.

By showing each character living a normal life, we connect with them. We recognise our own experiences in theirs. We start to walk in their shoes.

From Real World: Politicians often work to embody this type of presenter. For example, in the UK, our Members Of Parliament (MPs) often shift into a variety of everyman styles.

Sometimes this is as they speak on the campaign trail, where they aim to ingratiate themselves into the hearts (and voting patterns) of the electorate. They eagerly share run-of-the-mill stories of their upbringing that highlight how they really do understand normal challenges within normal lives.

Sometimes this is as they speak at the party conference. They stand at the lectern, surrounded by the branding of the party, talking the party language, invoking the party's history, portraying themselves as a core party loyalist.

Sometimes this is as they speak in the House of Commons. Many of the rituals and rules of the chamber are set down to keep a sense of respect and equality (not always successfully). For example, MPs are not referred to by their names, but by the name of the constituency that they represent.

Being your everyman prez-type sets you and each member of the audience as **equal members of a community**. You bring these people together. You remind people of **what binds them** together: aligned purpose, shared history, established traditions. All exist under one banner – the **identity** that defines who we are and what we do.

Everyman: **When to Select**

Choose to be an everyman prez-type when you want to unite your audience behind their shared values and beliefs and encourage them to work together for mutual success.

Select the everyman prez-type when you want to...

...build rapport with your audience.	You need key stakeholders to see you as part of their tribe (e.g. industry). You want to show that you use the same language, know the same people, share elements of history, have been part of the tribe's habits and practices. So they feel comfortable with you.	*e.g. You will present to a new client on your primary offering. They have not worked with your company before. You want them to see you as part of their industry.*
...hear from everyone.	You want to hear from your audience. You know they may have questions. You expect them to have experience to build on the plans you are sharing. You want to give everyone a chance to share their thoughts, from the least experienced voice to the most experienced voice.	*e.g. You will speak at the yearly strategy deployment day – to highlight how the plans build naturally on past work. You want everyone to have the chance to ask questions and add perspectives.*
...encourage the team to repeat existing processes.	You have a set of actions and an outcome in mind. You are confident that the team knows how to achieve both. You will emphasise the well-grooved habits and practices of the team. You will appeal to their sense of pride in being a group that gets things done in the right way, following established processes.	*e.g. You are briefing the consumer relations team on a product recall that may cause consumer complaints. The team knows how to respond to these – they know what to do and it is time for them to do it.*
...create a sense of collective responsibility.	You feel that everyone is integral to achieving a key outcome. You need everyone in the audience pulling in the same direction, fulfilling their important role in the mechanics of the plan. You want each member of the group to feel vital and you want everyone to trust others will do their bit.	*e.g. You are deploying an important brand launch. Success relies on Sales, Marketing, and Product Supply operating in careful collaboration. You need them working separately but collectively.*

Everyman **Task:** You are there to...

Check that you can focus on the right thing. The everyman prez-type is best when you want to...

...unite »

You **unite** the "tribe" behind a shared purpose. You **unite** them behind a common history. You **unite** them as equals: in voice and in responsibility.

...collaborate »

You **collaborate** with your audience to get things done. You **collaborate** with them to encourage them to work together. You **collaborate** with them to build trust.

As you unite the audience behind their common purpose and collaborate with them to achieve mutual success, you may consider one or more of the following:

assemble »
You call your audience together. You gather all to a consistent space. This place is your version of the village square, with its recognisable markers (tribe name, colours, emblem, etc.), sufficient seating for everyone, amenities to meet every member's basic needs, and the accoutrements of any traditions and routines.

listen »
You make sure that you stop talking and take the time to listen to your audience. You ensure that everyone, from the newest to the longest serving, has the opportunity to talk. Each voice, each perspective, is given equal weighting.

trust »
You trust the audience to work together towards a united goal. You trust them to support each other. You trust them to rely on each other. Each person brings individual talents and skills – these are brought together as vital cogs in the overall interconnected machine.

uphold »
You remind them that there are ways that we do things. There are standard ceremonies and familiar drills. You ensure these ways are followed. You maintain the procedures, practices, and routines of the tribe. This consistency gives people confidence to focus on what is to be done and their role in doing it.

Intensity of Everyman

 Mild   Medium   Hot

NEWBIE	EQUAL	COLLEAGUE	**ALLY**	FRIEND	KIN	**COMPATRIOT**

As an everyman prez-type you are there to uphold the interdependencies, rituals and traditions of the tribe, whether as a relative newcomer or the longest serving member.

When you are new to the group, eager to fit into the existing norms, select a **newbie-everyman**. When you are an experienced stalwart of the group, consider being an **ally-everyman**. When you are central elder of the group, whom others look to most to embody everything about the tribe, select a **compatriot-everyman**.

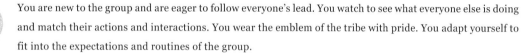

Mild-intensity

NEWBIE

You are new to the group and are eager to follow everyone's lead. You watch to see what everyone else is doing and match their actions and interactions. You wear the emblem of the tribe with pride. You adapt yourself to fit into the expectations and routines of the group.

Your audience will accept you easily. They recognise that you are working hard to fit in. Any time you don't quite do or say something correctly, they will kindly set you straight – showing you how they would do it.

Medium-intensity

ALLY

You are well integrated within the team. They know and trust you; you know and trust them. You are well versed in the habits and practices, the minor and major routines. You have their back and they know you have theirs.

Your audience quickly feels at ease with you. They see you as someone who understands their situation because you live it too.

Hot-intensity

COMPATRIOT

You epitomise what it means to be an active member of the tribe. You live and breathe the actions and activities, the routines and the ceremonies. You prioritise the needs of the tribe over your own hopes and wishes. You fulfil your role quickly and diligently, and then work hard to support others.

Your audience is inspired to frame everything within what is best for the group as a whole. They readily commit to fulfil their part of the plan. They feel blessed to be part a strong team.

Everyman: **Shape Sharpeners**

Tips on how to choose and arrange your content for a everyman type of presentation.

Hone Your Messaging

Make your main messages:

connections

A statement that reminds them of what ties us together and/or how we do things here.

A team name, moniker, mantra, characteristic, style, motto, strength, habit, profession.

e.g. *"Tous pour un, un pour tous" (All for one, and one for all)* The Three Musketeers.[31]

You want your audience to **trust** you and your message. Connect to what underpins the successes of the group. Maybe reference folkloric tales of the group's former successes (e.g. fabled case studies).

Find ways to **repeat** the message in a pattern or drumbeat. Integrate the message into the repeating routines of the group. Best if the audience themselves regularly recite the message themselves.

Shave Your Information

PRIORITISE

The **habits and routines** that bind the group together.

☆ Reiteration of the **purpose** of the group. What we stand for.

☆ Reinforcement of the power of **collective responsibility**. How we are each integral to the final outcome.

INCLUDE

✓ Existing best practices.

✓ Folklore stories from our shared past.

✓ Activities of people from within the group.

✓ Things that exemplify who we are and what we do.

✓ The many roles we play in achieving goals.

✓ Ideas and input from across the group.

DEPRIORITISE

The **external**.

✗ Outside perspectives and views.

✗ Questions on habits and practices.

✗ Novel processes and practices.

✗ Directives from outside of the group.

Great ways to
structure parts of
your presentation.

Three + Time Structure – Past, Present, and Future:

Section your content into three.

O Past – What we know and have established from our shared past.

O Present – What we know and our status today.

O Future – What we will do tomorrow to fulfil our responsibilities.

Time Structure – Custom Procedure:

Take your audience through the steps of the process, in chronological order.

O At the start, clarify the purpose of the procedure and emphasise its provenance.

O Walk through each step in the process.

O Pause at the end of each step to check people follow. Remind them of their individual roles and responsibilities (or ask for volunteers).

O At the end, again check for any questions on roles and process.

O Close by re-emphasising the overall purpose.

Time Structure – Origin Story:

Introduce a character from the group's past – ensure they are recognisable as emblematic of the "tribe". The habits and behaviours should reflect those of the group. Through the story, paint a picture of how an everyday member of the group found the set of values and customs that overcame the challenges that they faced. Describe how this character brought what they had learnt back into the tribe, solving for everyone a challenge that they used to face. End the story with how this process is now fully fixed into the best practices and expectations of the group.

Great ways to
open and close
your presentation.

Include in your opening: Set your connection to your audience. Find a way to reference your direct involvement with something unique to this tribe. Ideally, a personal story of you working directly with people within the community.

Include in your closing section: Remind them of our shared purpose and the traditional way we complete tasks. Reinforce how success is dependent on all of us playing our part. Consider re-enforcing the importance of the purpose and the success of the community.

Everyman: **Shift Keys**

Signal

**Indicate to
your audience
how to listen.**

Demonstrate early how you are connected to this group. Reference your relationship with people known by everyone in the room. Integrate terminology distinct to the group (e.g. industry terms). Be authentic and genuine, your audience needs to see you are comfortable with them. They want to be able to trust you and your motivations.

Signal that you are an equal member of the group; whatever your role and however high (or low) your rank, you are talking as a colleague, on a par with everyone in the team.

Spoken Language

Speak fairly plainly (or whatever is thought as plain to this audience). Talk of shared responsibility and mutual trust.

Use language common within the group: terms and terminology well understood by everyone. Use their vernacular (slang, acronyms, short names, etc.).

You frame things with "we" and "us" (rather than "I" or "they"). You reference directly people in the group using their first (given) names.

You find ways to bring the voices of the group into your presentation. Quote others. Invite them to speak.

Emotional language:

O You will likely speak **calmly**, in neutral tones.

O More heightened emotions may be aimed towards **admiration** for what we collectively achieve and **anticipation** for the continued teamwork.

Body Language

You should appear relaxed and comfortable with your audience. You are amongst friends and equals.

Your body language should mirror the body language of the group. Find ways to copy their postures and gestures. Or encourage them to follow yours.

Your gestures should be open – keen to show you are speaking to everyone equally.

You are drawn towards the audience as a whole. If the focus is on one individual, look to bring the attention back to everyone in the room.

Your clothing reflects the group; you are seen as one with the group. You may wear symbols of significance to the group e.g. logos, emblems etc. Avoid any clothing or symbols that imply a rank (high or low).

Staging

Lay out the room to maximise a sense of equality – everyone is of equal standing.

You want to be amongst the audience. If you must be separate (e.g. large stage) can you invite representatives from the audience to join you there?

Enter the room with everyone else. Be part of the audience for other presenters. Step out from the audience to start (and return when you finish).

Virtual: Encourage everyone to have their webcam on. Arrange so as many webcams as possible can be seen. Perhaps everyone uses the same virtual background? Organise so everyone is at their laptop.

Small room: Move the room around so everyone feels equal e.g. create a single circle of chairs with you in with them. Work to get even lighting across the group.

Large room: Work hard to create equality (often harder in larger rooms) e.g. bring everyone forward so all empty seats are at the back. Make the stage feel like a natural extension of their space rather than a separate stage area (i.e. remove obstacles).

Visuals

Use visuals and/or props that your audience will feel comfortable with; you want nothing too surprising or unusual.

Use local designs and colours. PowerPoint decks and other visuals are likely to rely heavily on team templates. Liberally use brand logos and mottos.

If using flip charts or whiteboards, choose colour carefully to match the tribe's identity.

Is there an object that is a symbol or mascot for the group? Can one be incorporated?

Try and include visuals from people in the audience e.g. photos of people, organograms, data from others. Ideally these could reinforce the sense of community by referring back to previous events (e.g. last year's deployment).

Utilise traditional music/group anthems that bring familiarity to the team or reflect the team's values/history.

How To Manage Your Presenter Notes

You feel very comfortable with your audience. They are equals and colleagues, not an audience to be intimidated by. Therefore it is absolutely fine to refer to notes as needed. Avoid reading a pre-prepared script – that suggests a higher or lower status. Use of a mind map is an excellent way to remind yourself of your structure and key points, without reading off detailed notes point by point.

If appropriate, give others the responsibility to make sure you have covered everything that you wanted to cover. Share an agenda of key points and ask the audience to confirm what has been covered and where to go next.

Their thoughts and perspectives must be represented. However, this is no time for a free-for-all. The traditions of the tribe should be maintained. No single voice should be given precedence. Therefore, you look to balance their autonomy and your control.

Freedom to give your audience

That stated, you are keen to hear many voices from across the audience. To highlight the equality across the room, ask first for thoughts and input from those who are newest to the group, then move onto the more experienced.

Remember that your prez-intent is set between actions and belonging. Keep discussions in these areas: what we will individually and collectively do plus how we will support each other in doing it.

Therefore:

O Crowdsource from the group: success stories, input on processes, etc.

O Ask for their commitments and to clarify support they need from others.

How? *Example processes include:*

O Ask for stories of how we have previously completed similar work in the past – *"Who has seen this before – what did we do and how did it work?"*

O Ask for input on how we might complete the work together – *"How might we do this? How would we split the work across the group?"*

O Ask for commitments for how they will each support the work – *"John – how will your team support this? What do you need from other groups?"*

Ready Yourself

☐ Find someone who you know well and who is well connected with the audience. Grab time with them to understand what people are chatting about. Are there any areas of friction? Any gentle gossip top of mind?

☐ Grab a piece of paper and note down:
　　　O What are the habits and practices that define us as a group?
　　　O Who do I know in the room? What shared experiences have we had?
　　　O What are key phrases that define the group?

☐ Get everything technically ready well in advance. You want to focus on being part of the audience before the presentation.

Everyman Prez-type **Watch Outs!**

Beware the dark side of the everyman prez-type. Avoid:

Stuck-in-the-Mud

Do not become so entrenched in the present norms that have got you this far, that you do not recognise the need to adapt to thrive in a changing world.

Echo Chamber

Avoid the trap of only welcoming voices from like-minded people so you never hear from others with diverse perspectives and experiences.

Handling likely objections: Acknowledge that some change may be important, but this will be through evolution rather than revolution. We will build first from what we know how to do well – we can make small changes from there.

Everyman Prez-type **Powerful Pairings**

Start as the **everyman** prez-type to re-establish yourself as one of the team. Then jump to the **explorer** prez-type, sharing new ideas and discoveries with the group. Then return to **everyman** prez-type to re-integrate new ideas into the group's established practices.

Start as **lover** prez-type to celebrate the amazing work delivered in the recent past. Then hop to the **everyman** prez-type to lay out the work that we will do next. Clarify individual roles and responsibilities. Set a sense of collective purpose.

Start as the **everyman** prez-type to layout your role in the traditions and norms of the group. Then something occurs that forces you into the **hero** prez-type. You are thrust forward to overcome dangerous challenges – success is vital to the group.

Tricky Transitions: Moving between **everyman** prez-type and **student** prez-type or **magician** prez-type will undermine your claim to be a group member. Your audience needs to see you as equally versed in their ways, so you cannot be an external learner (**student**) or be imbued with power well beyond them (**magician**).

Caregiver

As a **caregiver** prez-type you guide progress and provide guardrails.

Caregiver

attendant

sentry

coach

guide

shepherd

governor

guardian

As a caregiver-type presenter you **guide** your audience. You support them through choices and actions. You **provide what they need** (not necessarily what they want!) to achieve their objectives.

You are responsible for the **health and well-being** of a group, most typically the audience. You have the authority to step in where needed to **protect** them. The audience feels **secure** and therefore able to get on with their actions, priorities, responsibilities, etc.

The Essence of the Caregiver

From Fiction: Mary Poppins is a classic example of a character that firmly guides the behaviour of the children in her care by setting clear expectations alongside firm boundaries to keep them protected. She introduces the children to the world of imagination and magic, while maintaining order and discipline. Her guidelines for the children (and their parents) are based not on what they want, but on what they need.

In the Chronicles of Narnia books, Aslan's character is a caregiver for the children. He sets expectations for the children's behaviour, providing moral guidance and emotional support, while actively working to keep them safe and protected in this unfamiliar land.

From Real World: If you have ever gone scuba diving, you will have experienced the divemaster giving you a briefing beforehand. They want you to have fun down in the deep blue sea, but they are setting definite parameters for the dive, ensuring all safety protocols are followed. The tone of this presentation is crucial – kind but firm.

We work with the Institute of Grocery Distribution (IGD) in the UK, who run big trade briefings for the major retailers. These events can have two thousand delegates sat ready to hear from important retail leaders. Guy Ousey, from the IGD, often acts as the host. He is a master at opening the event. He sets everyone at ease (including the other speakers) and he guides everyone on highlights to look out for. He will brief on important safety information and logistics like how the lunch break will work. His role at this point is to give everyone the information they need, so they can relax into listening to the speakers they have come to hear.

> *"Leadership is not about being in charge. It's about taking care of those in your charge."*
> Simon Sinek

Being your caregiver prez-type allows you to **guide actions and expectations**, to be clear on what you want to happen. This is done in the context of trust and respect for your audience; you want them to be safe, to be protected, so you **form guardrails** to make sure they come to no harm.

Caregiver: **When to Select**

Choose to be a caregiver prez-type when you want your audience to proceed confidently to accomplish a task or achieve a goal. They feel safe and secure in what to do, and what not to do.

Select the caregiver prez-type when you want to...

...brief on a process to follow.	You have a set of steps that they need to follow. By complying, they avoid possible difficulties. They do not need to understand the whys and wherefores of the process. They need to know enough to complete the process to achieve their aim.	*e.g. You are leading vital qualitative research. You have a group of VIP visitors to brief: to explain how they can observe without affecting the research.*
...advise a group on how to achieve a goal.	You are supporting a team of people to reach their own goals. You have experience and expertise, and are there to guide how they move forward. They are not looking for your opinion on why things are so, they need your guiding hand on how to progress.	*e.g. You need to make a final presentation on a consulting project. You are leaving the client with next steps to maintain progress.*
...save a team from making damaging mistakes.	You need to intervene. A team, possibly a lead team, has a plan of action that will lead to significant failure, catastrophic damage, or similar. They need you to intercede, to step forward, briefly layout what is about to happen, and firmly guide them back to a safe path.	*e.g. You are the legal counsel. Your lead team has just confirmed a plan that you believe will go against local laws. You call an urgent meeting to ensure all decisions are paused and a review put in place.*
...guide a partnering team through a difficult path.	You are supporting a team who have concerns about their plan. There is something about the strategy and process that means it feels difficult and risky. They want you to clarify the path they should follow, and for you to set guardrails to ensure their safety, and to take their hand as they step tentatively through the key steps.	*e.g. You are guiding a team through the final testing of a business-critical IT system. They are paranoid about missing code issues. You explain how each step in the testing process gives the chance of finding any issues.*

Caregiver **Task:** You are there to...

Check that you can focus on the right thing. The caregiver prez-type is best when you want to...

...guide »

You **guide** their expectations on what they can achieve. You **guide** the route they should follow. You **guide** the steps they should take.

...protect »

You **protect** them from ill-advised actions. You **protect** them from unforeseeable dangers. You **protect** them from drops in energy and focus.

As you guide their progress and provide guardrails, you may consider one or more of the following:

coach »

You train your audience in a capability. Push your audience through defined practice steps and exercises. Check their progress by providing feedback. You develop their key skills and behaviours.

shepherd »

You lead your "flock" through vital gates and into connecting fields. You are confident this is where they need to go, and that you can get them there safely. From time to time you pause, allow the audience to digest the information, before moving them on to the next field.

reassure »

You temper any concerns. You embolden your audience through transparent parameters and guidelines. You confirm that if they follow the outlined approach, and stick to the established guardrails, they will achieve their objective.

sustain »

You support your audience as they progress towards their objective. You aid their progress. This can be practical advice, physical backing, or moral support. The assistance can be directly from you, or indirectly through others.

Intensity of Caregiver

 Mild   Medium   Hot

| ATTENDANT | SENTRY | COACH | **GUIDE** | SHEPHERD | GOVERNOR | **GUARDIAN** |

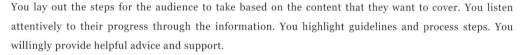

As a caregiver prez-type an important element is how the audience sees you. To them, you may be a "helping hand", or a "guiding hand", or a "supervising hand".

When the audience considers you a support they can call upon, select an **attendant-caregiver**. When they need you to collaboratively coach them through the content, select the **guide-caregiver**. If you have a responsibility for their welfare, especially if there are real dangers present, select a **guardian-caregiver**.

Mild-intensity

ATTENDANT

You lay out the steps for the audience to take based on the content that they want to cover. You listen attentively to their progress through the information. You highlight guidelines and process steps. You willingly provide helpful advice and support.

The audience feels enabled and empowered to work through information and activities. You highlight when anyone makes a mistake or miscomprehends a step, especially if it might put someone in danger.

Medium-intensity

GUIDE

You advise the audience throughout to deliver their objectives in line with expectations. You shepherd them away from unnecessary risks. You appraise their present understanding and adapt your guidance based on what they need most.

The audience trusts you to collaboratively support them. You give regular check steps and feedback. You will intervene when your skills will assist.

Hot-intensity

GUARDIAN

You supervise throughout the presentation. You are responsible for their well-being and their progress. You are calm and caring, but you set defined boundaries on how you will share information, processes, etc. You actively monitor how everyone is progressing through the presentation.

Whenever you see fit, you step in to ensure everyone is where they should be, and doing what they should be doing. As long as they are, you step back again to allow them to focus on the information that you are sharing.

Caregiver: **Shape Sharpeners**

Tips on how to choose and arrange your content for a caregiver type of presentation.

Hone Your Messaging

Make your main messages:

guidance

Ensure it is **clear** not only **what they need** to do, but also provide **reassurance** that you are **there to support** them in achieving their goal.

A forewarning, piece of advice, technique, pathway, intervention, guideline.

e.g. *"There are six emergency exits on this aircraft. Take a minute to locate the exit closest to you. Note that the nearest exit may be behind you."*

Ensure your motives and experience are **trusted**. Show that you have their best interests in mind. Reference your experience in supporting people on this topic.

Ensure your messages are **simple**. Concisely lay out the steps to be taken. Include risks that should be avoided.

Calmly **repeat** guiding instructions. Make these available at any time the audience need them during and after your presentation e.g. poster, handout, handbook, QR code for website, expert on hand.

Shave Your Information

PRIORITISE

The **outcomes** and their **safe** progress.

☆ **Expectations:** outline of what they (and you) expect them to achieve.

☆ **Guardrails.** Protection that is in place so they can proceed confidently.

INCLUDE

✓ Guidelines to follow.

✓ Overview of the path, with details on each step.

✓ Elements that build trust in you and the process.

✓ Hazard warnings.

✓ Where they can get further info, if they need it.

DEPRIORITISE

The **undermining**.

✗ Risk that hasn't been mitigated against.

✗ Info that undercuts your status.

✗ Details that over explain.

✗ Contradicting options or ideas.

Great ways to structure parts of your presentation.

Three Structure – Three-Step Instruction:

Give your audience three things, concisely stated. These may be actions to take, things to look out for, deadlines to hit e.g. *"Mirror, signal, manoeuvre"* is a classic direction from a driving instructor to encourage a learner to use their rear-view mirror before turning.

This is enough to feel comprehensive (covers what is needed) while still only using a few things for them to process and remember (keeping them confident they can keep up).

Three Structure – Fairy-tale Trio:

This guides your audience from comfort, through uncertainty, and finally to safety.

1) **The prize:** what the audience is focussed on. Their wishes and aspirations. They confidently follow a well-worn path (Little Red Riding Hood) or tentatively step into the unknown with a flawed protection process (Hansel and Gretel with the breadcrumbs eaten by birds).

2) **The wolf or the witch:** what the audience is blissfully unaware of. Hazards, pitfalls, dangers. Or swindlers, tricksters, crooks.

3) **The supported escape:** what the audience should do to navigate safely through the hazards to a successful outcome (Little Red and Hansel and Gretel get away). Normally enabled by a protecting figure (e.g. woodsman or white duck/swan).

News Structure – Continue Until Clear:

State first the big idea that you want to convey; why what you are saying is important and should be listened to. Then summarise the key expectations and instructions. Then give a few lower-level details, but not more than needed. Keep check-stepping their understanding and comfort. Once they are clear, you stop. All further details can be provided in a handout (perhaps with a pre-prepared Frequently Asked Questions sheet).

Great ways to open and close your presentation.

Include in your opening: Be clear that you will be laying out guidelines for their actions. Emphasise your understanding of what they are trying to achieve. Mention that guardrails are there to keep everyone safe. Take the time to build up trust with your audience so they can see you care about them collectively and as individuals.

Include in your closing section: A summary of the guidelines for them to follow, reminder of any major hazards, and where people can go to get more information and support if they have any questions.

Caregiver: **Shift Keys**

Signal

Indicate to your audience how to listen.

Indicate your role as caregiver and guide. Tell them from the start that you are there to help and to support them. Maybe add a process that shows you are keen to understand their situation and what they need – collectively and individually. This includes their comfort needs (food, water, warmth, etc.) as well as their higher needs (achievements, goals, etc.).

Follow this with a firmer message: that there are rules that must be followed, and these are for everyone's safety and security. Highlight that there are dangers and risks.

Spoken Language

Choose warm and inclusive language. Show that you care about them collectively and individually. Be encouraging, but don't praise too highly.

Talk calmly and kindly. Your tone is going to be soft, with a firmness when needed, and smooth in volume and pace. You do not want to startle them.

Speak clearly (articulate well) as you share any safety rules, guidelines, instructions, etc. Use language that everyone can understand, including those least knowledgeable or adept.

Regularly check for understanding before moving on.

Emotional language:

○ Express emotions around **fear** for their welfare and **anticipation** of their progress.

○ You may communicate **sadness**, and even **disgust**, if they do something dangerous.

Body Language

Your body language is a sort of contradiction. You stand tall (so you can see everyone and everyone can see you) but also keep yourself contained (to seem less intimidating).

Gestures are warm, such as opening your arms to metaphorically circle your audience. Your movements are smooth. You avoid sharp gestures – you want to steer clear of anything that frightens your audience.

You dress in a similar way to your audience, although perhaps on the slightly more formal side. You convey that directions need to be followed, that you retain the right to intervene. Your clothing may include signals as to why you should be trusted e.g. symbols that demonstrate your experience, your role to protect, and your responsibility for their welfare.

Staging

You must be visible, easily seen by all of the audience. Additionally, ensure you can see everyone so that you can help anyone who has questions, or is struggling (or not listening).

Maybe place chairs in a curve around the stage space. Place those who will need most help closest to you (and the most independent furthest away).

Create a base station for yourself where you see all of the audience, they can find you before and after, and you can keep all your resources and materials.

Position yourself at the centre of the space at the start. Be close, but not too close, to your audience; make sure they can hear you clearly. When you give them time to reflect or try things themselves, step back to supervise from a distance.

 Virtual: Spotlight your webcam so all see you clearly. Set webcam so you look accessible and calming.

 Small room: Good if they are all sat and you stand (watching over). Seat them in small groups (e.g. chairs in pairs/threes).

 Large room: Look to make everyone feel safe. Seating in cabaret (chairs around tables) if possible.

Visuals

Visuals need to be clear and concise. Include process/method diagrams.

Find ways to demonstrate any procedures. Even better if you include ways for them to practise processes themselves – to see themselves and others successfully following protocols.

The most vital information (e.g. safety guidelines) should be available throughout (e.g. on a poster).

Keep visuals unexceptional – neither too big or grand, nor too rough or spontaneous.

Visuals need to be calming yet firm. Use reds and oranges for warnings; bold black for key guidelines, and more muted shades/hues for everything else.

Form materials that will be easy for them to find after the presentation (e.g. handout or URL). Prioritise materials that reinforce core instructions, offer answers to standard questions, and provide ways that people can find out the answers to any further questions later.

Care must be given to the accuracy of the information, there should be no opportunity for doubt.

How To Manage Your Presenter Notes

You are highly likely (and it is absolutely acceptable) to refer to carefully pre-prepared notes; it is imperative the guidance and instructions shared are complete and correct. You are guiding their actions away from dead ends and around hazards – it is best to check you have covered everything. Probably avoid a full script, but detailed notes are sensible, whether in a series of mind maps or as a checklist on your computer.

Interact

You need to maintain sufficient control to ensure the group feels protected, but still free to work with the information you share. Therefore, the level of control you require depends on the dangers involved. Sometimes you hold them back and sometimes you let them go.

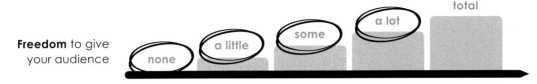

Freedom to give your audience — none · a little · some · a lot · total

You want responses that confirm they understand and can safely try things. Activities may include facilitated practice that shows actions can be successfully (safely) completed.

Therefore:

O Brief the audience at the start on how you will interact with them to gather questions or confirm their understanding.

O Ask check questions where they respond when they understand (i.e. "raise your hand if that was clear" and not "raise your hand if that was unclear"). This way you check who is unclear or was not listening to your question.

O Adapt your interaction to the needs of individuals. Set tasks for those feeling assured, while you focus on those who most need your assistance.

O Consider pre-briefing potential coaches in the audience e.g. managers of groups within the audience. These people will cascade the guidance to others during and after your presentation. They may be the most experienced, or the most senior, but sometimes are simply key influencers in the group.

How? *Example processes include:*

O Check the instructions are understood – *"Please put your hand up to confirm you understand what you now need to do?"*

O Open questions – *"Does anyone have any questions before we proceed?"*

O Guided practice – *"Please complete step three – I will give you feedback afterwards."*

Ready Yourself

☐ It is extremely important to convey a sense of calm confidence. So, take the time to settle yourself before you come in. Focus on deep breathing exercises. Do gentle stretches and balance exercises to get yourself grounded (good posture). Do vocal exercises to get control of your voice.

☐ Set up a base station for yourself in the room. A place where you have everything that you need, and where you can be found by anyone with questions.

☐ Double-check that any guided practices will work. Have you got all of the equipment you need – is there the space to do them?

The Versatile Presenter

Caregiver Prez-type **Watch Outs!**

Beware the dark side of the caregiver prez-type. Avoid:

Inadvertently Infantilise

"Helping people" can morph into "stifling people".
At some point you need to loosen the apron strings and offer them freedom to explore on their own.

Backseat Driver

Not all feedback is seen as constructive. Not every coach is seen as credible. Be ready to share how your guidance is well intentioned and based on experience.

Handling likely objections: The danger is people feeling patronised and constrained. Help them understand how you will guide and support them, but that they are in control. You will only be forceful when it is to protect them from serious risks. Otherwise, you are there to help when and how they choose.

Caregiver Prez-type **Powerful Pairings**

 Start as the **ruler** prez-type, establishing the direction and directing the action. Once the instructions have been clearly communicated you hop to the **caregiver** prez-type, showing care and consideration for the well-being of your audience.

 Begin as the **explorer** prez-type to travel through the exciting new information. Once the audience starts to feel uncertain of how discoveries can be applied, jump to **caregiver** prez-type, to guide them through how things will work in practice.

 Set up the need for change as the **hero** prez-type: outline the risks of inertia, admit to the challenges they face. The audience becomes inspired but hesitant. Calmly jump to be the **caregiver** prez-type: provide reassurance and guidance on what the audience now needs to do and how they will be protected.

 Tricky Transitions: Moving between **caregiver** prez-type and **sage** prez-type or **maverick** prez-type breaks their sense of security. You need them to trust your guidance, but this is cracked if you then revel in theoretical debates (**sage**) or then rail against established routines and regulations (**maverick**).

Ruler

As a **ruler** prez-type you establish direction and direct action.

Ruler

gatekeeper

warden

conductor

maestro

director

head

sovereign

As a ruler-type presenter you **verify your authority to direct** them, coming either through the scope of your role, or through your standing, or through orders set by a higher authority.

You **establish what you expect of them**: objectives, commitments, and targets. You **direct their actions** and track progress.

The audience recognises, and often appreciates, that someone has **decided what must be done** and briefs them on what they must do and by when.

The Essence of the Ruler

> "The challenge of leadership is to be strong, but not rude; be kind, but not weak; be bold, but not bully; be thoughtful, but not lazy; be humble, but not timid; be proud, but not arrogant; have humour, but without folly."
>
> Jim Rohn

From Fiction: Rulers often get a bad reputation in fiction, portrayed as cruel and tyrannical. Joffrey Baratheon (*Game of Thrones*) and President Snow (*The Hunger Games*) are narcissistic despots. But look again and you do find wise and compassionate rulers: Aragorn (*The Lord of the Rings*), Captain Picard (*Star Trek*), M (*James Bond*), Roz (*Monsters Inc.*).

Whether cruel or compassionate, each ruler sets direction and makes hard decisions. Dumbledore (headmaster of Hogwarts) lays down rules and makes both popular and unpopular calls, from hiring staff to allowing the Tri-Wizard tournament to go ahead.

Not all rulers are high-ranking "leaders". You can "rule" your own small domain. You can enforce rules set by others. In the James Bond movies, Moneypenny is not the boss, but you only get in to see M if she allows it.

From Real World: An audience responds well to having an authority, whom they respect as fair and just, make clear what is expected of them. A head presenting to staff about learning targets for the year, respected because of their role as leader of the school.

However, you do not need to be a leader to use this prez-type. It is about having defined goals and stated directions, backed by an acknowledged authority. A manager connecting the team's progress on the action plan to the company's goals. A speaker summarising new rules and regulations for country sporting bodies, relying on the authority of the International Olympic Committee. A finance manager reviewing business results with the executive team, reminding them of targets they set themselves for the year.

Being your ruler prez-type gives you the right tone to **set direction**, to be crystal **clear on objectives and goals**: what they need to do and by when. You may give them the autonomy to work out exactly how they deliver against the targets. You track and rate progress. You **give prizes and hand out penalties**.

 # Ruler: **When to Select**

Choose to be a ruler prez-type when you need to make sure your audience are certain of the actions they are to take and resolved to execute them effectively and efficiently.

Select the ruler prez-type when you want to...

...set the direction for a major strategy intervention.	You have something to convey to your audience. You have done the thinking, the decisions are made, and now is the time to deploy the action steps. You are not open to influence and you will convey assuredness and decisiveness. You expect the plan to be executed.	*e.g. You are briefing the organisation on office changes. You are combining office locations, which requires the relocation of many employees and the redundancy of others.*
...co-ordinate an event which is reliant on many participants.	You are responsible for a plan which requires the synchronisation of many moving parts. Everybody involved must appreciate enough about the overall programme to ensure they execute their responsibilities in a timely manner. Each aspect must dovetail with all other elements for the programme to be delivered.	*e.g. You are running a major conference. You are to brief speakers on how the event will work: logistics for the attendees, timings for rehearsals, technical details (like microphones), and more.*
...project-manage a multifunctional initiative.	The success of your project relies on people working together efficiently, bringing together their knowledge, expertise and collaborative skills to deliver the plan. You need to ensure each individual understands the action they need to make to contribute to the overall success.	*e.g. You are presenting to the team on a brand re-launch that you lead. You must co-ordinate all aspects including planning, production, sales and marketing.*
...ensure strict implementation of a new procedure.	You have been given responsibility for making sure an agreed process or procedure is followed. You did not necessarily contribute to, or approve, the plan, but it is your responsibility to ensure it is implemented correctly.	*e.g. You need to implement a new financial discipline to your sales teams. You announce that invoices will no longer be paid unless they are processed correctly.*

Ruler **Task:** You are there to...

Check that you can focus on the right thing. The ruler prez-type is best when you want to...

...establish »

You **establish** the authority involved (yours or from a separate source). You **establish** the decisions. You **establish** the objectives and targets.

...direct »

You **direct** them on priorities for a set of actions.
You **direct** them towards upcoming checks and gates.
You **direct** them to update you on progress.

As you are establishing the direction and directing the action, you may consider one or more of the following:

state »

You express directives with clarity, authority and a sense of purpose. You brief them on goals, gates, criteria, rules, and more. There is no doubt in your plan of action. The decisions have been made.

supervise »

You oversee the implementation of the plan. You may establish systems and processes to track and measure implementation of the plan. You may delegate specific responsibilities or actions, expecting timely briefings or reports. You retain ultimate authority.

conduct »

You manage the implementation of the plan. You may establish systems and processes to track and measure implementation of the plan. You may delegate specific responsibilities or actions, expecting timely briefings or reports. You retain ultimate authority.

govern »

You ensure the governance framework, rules and regulations are adhered to. You highlight opportunities for improvement when this will be beneficial to the overall directive. You penalise transgressions fairly but firmly.

Intensity of Ruler

Mild   Medium   Hot

GATEKEEPER   WARDEN   CONDUCTOR   **MAESTRO**   DIRECTOR   HEAD   **SOVEREIGN**

The variation in your ruler prez-type comes from your audience's perception of your innate authority.

When you are tasked with overseeing rules and regulations set by someone else, select a **gatekeeper-ruler**. When you have clear authority to co-ordinate, select the **maestro-ruler**. If you have the highest authority minds of the audience, where they are extremely keen to meet your every request, select a **sovereign-ruler**.

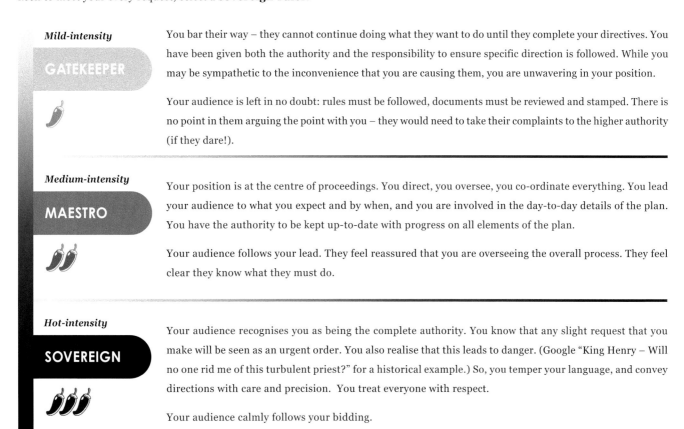

Mild-intensity
GATEKEEPER

You bar their way – they cannot continue doing what they want to do until they complete your directives. You have been given both the authority and the responsibility to ensure specific direction is followed. While you may be sympathetic to the inconvenience that you are causing them, you are unwavering in your position.

Your audience is left in no doubt: rules must be followed, documents must be reviewed and stamped. There is no point in them arguing the point with you – they would need to take their complaints to the higher authority (if they dare!).

Medium-intensity
MAESTRO

Your position is at the centre of proceedings. You direct, you oversee, you co-ordinate everything. You lead your audience to what you expect and by when, and you are involved in the day-to-day details of the plan. You have the authority to be kept up-to-date with progress on all elements of the plan.

Your audience follows your lead. They feel reassured that you are overseeing the overall process. They feel clear they know what they must do.

Hot-intensity
SOVEREIGN

Your audience recognises you as being the complete authority. You know that any slight request that you make will be seen as an urgent order. You also realise that this leads to danger. (Google "King Henry – Will no one rid me of this turbulent priest?" for a historical example.) So, you temper your language, and convey directions with care and precision. You treat everyone with respect.

Your audience calmly follows your bidding.

 # Ruler: **Shape Sharpeners**

Tips on how to choose and arrange your content for a ruler type of presentation.

Hone Your Messaging

Make your main messages:

directives

Every message will be **concise and crystal clear.** You deliver a **statement of expected actions.**

Goals, targets, actions, outcomes, results, rules, demands, expectations.

e.g. *"Stay Home, Protect the NHS, Save Lives"* UK Government message during COVID.

Ensure your message is **simple**. Make it straightforward and direct. You know that complexity and unnecessary details lead to indecision and confusion.

Repeat your message regularly throughout your presentation. Say it early, say it frequently, and end with it. Reinforce by repeating it in other forms: slides, handouts, emails, etc. Leave them in no doubt that this is the message they must take away.

Shave Your Information

PRIORITISE

Things to be done.

☆ **Targets and objectives.** Simple statement of expected outcomes.

☆ **Prioritised actions.** What comes first, second, and after.

INCLUDE

✓ Overview of the plan, focussing on tracking gates.

✓ Elements that reinforce the origin of your authority.

✓ Brief rationale or purpose behind the directive.

✓ Reference (or inference) of potential prizes and penalties.

DEPRIORITISE

The **superfluous**.

✗ Explanation beyond what is needed: minor details, fun facts, etc.

✗ Unnecessary validation of your authority.

✗ Exploration of other options considered.

Chart Your Structure

Great ways to structure parts of your presentation.

One Structure – A Single, Simple Directive:

The best way to ensure an action is executed is to state it as a single idea – do this! Say it early and say it often. Repetition can reinforce this idea, using words, visuals, handouts – but a simple single idea will help to ensure the audience are **sure on actions** they are to take and **resolved to execute them** effectively and efficiently.

Time Structure – Critical Path:

Work chronologically step-by-step through the plans. At each time point, cover things like

1) Remind people of objectives and goals.

2) Lay out overall plan for each section.

3) Update on progress.

4) Confirm next steps and roles and responsibilities.

Two Structure – Carrot and Stick:

An audience is used to weighing up pros and cons, and when following directives, they like to know the benefits of compliance and the damages of non-compliance. We prefer the prizes to be generous and the penalties to be minor, but it depends on the presentation scenario. Categorise your content into these two areas:

1) The prize you will hand out for success (or compliance). The actions expected and the targets to be reached. The prizes available.

2) The penalty you will hand out for failure. The lowest acceptable results. The prohibited actions or behaviours that will be penalised.

Note: Fairness is vital when using the ruler prez-type. Therefore, both your prizes and penalties must be balanced, reasonably attainable by all involved, and honestly judged.

Great ways to open and close your presentation.

Include in your opening: Set the expectation that you will share directions that they will need to follow. Tell them that you will provide clear instructions for the audience's deliverables and actions. Reference the source of your authority e.g. decision from lead team meeting, target set by executive, the mission statement of the company, a relevant law, a rule set by a regulatory body, the responsibility given to you, etc.

Include in your closing section: A clear and concise reinforcement of the expected action.

Ruler: **Shift Keys**

Signal

Indicate to your audience how to listen.

Have in view the symbol of your authority and what you have authority over. In some situations there is clothing (referee outfit) or an object (e.g. whistle, flag, or conductor's baton). Where they apply, include decorations that highlight the authority – banners, standards, etc.

Place yourself centre stage or in the highest position (e.g. umpire chair). Start with a solemn tone and a calm, assured manner. Treat everyone consistently – firm but fair with everyone, from the highest ranking to the lowest ranking person.

 Spoken Language

You will use precise, prepared (maybe scripted), and formal language.

Use direct language (e.g. *"You will..."* rather than *"I'd like you to..."*). Sentences are short and to the point.

Language should be kept simple: understandable by everyone involved in executing the plan.

Language explains what is to be achieved. It likely includes by whom and by when.

You are very comfortable with pauses. You will speak in your own time and at your own pace. You use pauses to pull their focus to you.

Emotional language:

O Keep **calm** but firm.

O You feel **anticipation** for their compliance.

 Body Language

Everything about your body should reflect authority: a composed poise. Accept within yourself that you are taking the higher status.

At key times, carefully share eye contact equally around all parts of the audience: before you start (pausing as you do); when you are setting rules and expectation.

Stand tall and upright, with your chest and head held high. Stand directly facing your audience (chest above hips, above feet, all facing out to your audience).

You are likely to stand still in one spot. Movements will be deliberate, slow, clear and controlled.

Gestures are often with palms down (and avoid with palms up). Avoid direct pointing (keep fingers together).

Dress formally: a suit, smart dress and jacket, or uniform. Ruler-like colours: black, deep red, purple.

Staging

Set out the room and lighting for a formal feel. There should be space between your position (centre "stage") and the audience.

Perhaps have imagery of your authority (e.g. corporate logo, team flag, company mission statements, etc.) visible behind you.

The audience is sat down first, ready for your arrival. You may be introduced by someone else. You arrive exactly on time and are ready to go.

You will make a formal entrance. You will take centre stage. You might be elevated or you might be sat (like a judge in a court or an umpire in tennis).

Virtual: Ensure your webcam is set at (or slightly below) your eye level. Angle so your head is central and touching the top of the frame. Have a formal backdrop. Prioritise a sound check beforehand.

Small room: If sat, sit at the head of the table. If stood, create a defined space in front of the audience. Ensure there is space for you to stand centre stage.

Large room: Create a raised stage space at the front. Seating in rows (theatre style) is appropriate.

Visuals

Visuals, if used at all, are simple and impactful. Either basic (do the job and no more) or highly designed (official visuals, probably created by someone else).

Try to use visuals with high contrast (i.e. avoid similar pastel sets) – this ensures everyone sees the information equally and reinforces confidence.

Pre-prepared materials, e.g. posters, convey permanence and assuredness (versus creating imagery live on a flip chart).

Everything must run smoothly. Technology (e.g. slides) may be progressed by someone else.

Targets to be reached are represented vividly. Key progress gates are visualised, perhaps in a timeline. Details of defined processes are available (e.g. QR code or handout), but probably not included as part of your content. An org chart may clarify the primary decision maker (you or the person giving you the authority).

Consider handouts for important information that they will refer to and take away: critical path, rules and regulations, priority actions, progress report, etc.

How To Manage Your Presenter Notes

It is important you are seen to get the information right, so your presentation may be scripted (possibly significantly). It is acceptable to be seen to refer to notes, you may even use an autocue. Whatever you use, make sure your notes are seen to have been carefully prepared (no scraps of paper with last minute scribbles!).

That stated, when you want to emphasise your authority, speaking confidently without notes does this best.

Interact

The ruler prez-type is not open to discussion and debate. Interactions likely focus on checking the audience is clear on your directives and your expectations.

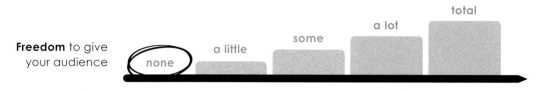

Freedom to give your audience: none (circled), a little, some, a lot, total

You expect responses that confirm their commitment.

Therefore:

○ Decide in advance if you will be taking questions or checking for understanding.

○ Be clear on how people will be allowed to respond (e.g. questions in chat or by Q&A application). Ensure execution will be smooth (have a technical check). Perhaps, delegate the process to someone else (you focus on choosing which questions to answer).

○ Be ready to be firm. If absolutely pushed, guide people to a separate process for questions e.g. *"This decision has already been taken. If you need to understand more about why, please contact Rebecca Morrison, our Vice President, directly through her office."*

How? *Example processes include:*

○ Check the instructions are understood – *"Hands up if you are in any way unsure of what is expected of you."*

○ Pre-prepared Q&A – *"I understand there are questions around the first week, John is handing out a briefing document that explains the plans fully."*

○ Request for public updates on progress and commitments – *"Ann, is your team on track to deliver by the end of the month as per the plan?"*

Ready Yourself

☐ Take the time to be calm before you come in. Focus on deep breathing exercises and vocal exercises to get control of your voice. Work the lower register of your voice (e.g. hum scales downwards, tapping your sternum as you do so to focus the sound into your chest).

☐ Do stretches and balance exercises to get yourself grounded (good posture with feet set). Do gentle shoulder and neck stretches.

☐ Ensure you know the room layout: how you will enter the stage and where centre stage will be.

☐ Know how the technology works, if you are going to be managing it yourself. Be comfortable with any microphone arrangements.

☐ Do NOT fidget.

Ruler Prez-type **Watch Outs!**

Beware the dark side of the ruler prez-type. Avoid:

Justification Junky

You must stay confident in decisions, rules, and targets. You will undermine confidence if you excessively explain the rationale and thinking behind things.

Despotism

BUT if you avoid any justification for your directives, people will feel bullied. If you only focus on penalties for failure, you lose support (and compliance).

Handling likely objections: The danger is always mutiny. They must feel you have the right to be in charge and that you will be fair-minded. Ensure it is clear that you have the authority to direct them. Be irrefutably balanced in how you direct them (and be comfortable to guide them to the formal appeals process if they have concerns).

Ruler Prez-type **Powerful Pairings**

Start as the **magician**, laying out the visionary strategy that will drive us forward. Then walk calmly to centre stage to become the **ruler** prez-type, laying out vital targets and expected actions – so people know what they are to do.

Start as the **hero** prez-type, sharing the noble cause we are fighting for and calling out the vital risks that we are taking. Then jump to **ruler** prez-type to set out instructions on who needs to do what and by when.

Start as the **ruler** prez-type, setting out the plan. Once the directives have been clearly communicated, you hop over to become the **caregiver** prez-type, showing how they can safely complete their responsibilities.

Tricky Transitions: Moving between **ruler** prez-type and **explorer** prez-type or **jester** prez-type makes it hard to maintain authority. You need everyone to stick to a plan and take things seriously, which you will undermine if you then choose to fly here, there and everywhere (**explorer**) or encourage playful irreverence (**jester**).

Creator

As a **creator** prez-type you eagerly demonstrate the usefulness of your creation.

Creator

draughtswoman

co-ordinator

builder

inventor

designer

craftsperson

artisan

As a creator-type presenter you **display** the thing that you have made. You highlight the problem that it solves – the important thing it helps the user to accomplish. You **explain how it works**.

You **enable them to use it**. You **demonstrate it working**. You enthuse at its **functionality** (and, possibly, its aesthetic). You **instruct** them on **how to use it effectively**. You leave them with materials with further instructions to follow.

The Essence of the Creator

From Fiction: Consider Q (short for Quartermaster) in the James Bond series. Q provides, slightly begrudgingly, the high-tech gadgetry that will enable Bond to complete the mission.

Remember Edna Mode from Pixar's *The Incredibles* ("*No capes!*"). She has painstakingly created bespoke superhero suits to harness the specific powers (and mitigate for the implications) of each member of the family. She has crafted perfect outfits, but holds no desire to wear a suit herself.

Sometimes the creation is a plan. In *Ocean's 11*, Danny Ocean has created an intricate plan to achieve the near-impossible casino heist. But he needs the other ten to have any hope of putting the plan into action.

"We cannot predict the future, but we can invent it."
Dennis Gabor[32]

From Real World: Few creations need to be truly groundbreaking. Many everyday inventions still need to be introduced to an audience e.g. the recipe for the perfect lasagne, presented by the TV chef on your favourite cooking programme.

From our working world: A training session on the updated process for maintaining a production line. A presentation covering a new computer application. A medical conference talk on an improved procedure for a standard operation. A big pitch presentation where the saleswoman walks through the details for how the big idea will work in practice.

Being your creator prez-type helps you **explain how something works** and **how someone can use it**. You have, in some way, **been instrumental in creating it**: you may have painstakingly built it from the ground up, or you may have only added a final flourish. Either way, you **put your creation centre stage** and demonstrate (and admire) the elegant way it **enables important things to be done**.

Creator: **When to Select**

Choose to be a creator prez-type when you want to show your audience how something works, why it works, and enable them to use it appropriately.

Select the creator prez-type when you want to...

...deploy a tool.	You have developed a new tool (e.g. application) to fix a known issue. You introduce it, demonstrate how it works, and highlight benefits versus current solutions. You offer to train their staff to enable implementation.	*e.g. You have developed an improved application to track production issues. You are to present this to the production team.*
...offer a new product or service.	You are introducing a new service to your key client that you are confident meets a key need of theirs. You show the innovative features (perhaps of a prototype) and demonstrate its functionality. You explain how they can integrate it into present processes to help hit the client's priority goals.	*e.g. You are explaining a new recruitment service to an engineering client. It should speed up sourcing specialists in mathematical modelling – a key priority of theirs.*
...optimise a process.	You are responsible for an important business procedure. You require input and assessment from an audience of stakeholders. You will work methodically through the existing method, collecting feedback and comments from the audience as you go.	*e.g. You lead a project to review how innovation is managed in the company. You are leading a workshop presentation with all the functional heads, to gather their thoughts on each step.*
...develop a strategic partnership.	You propose collaboration ideas that leverage the complementary strengths and resources of potential partners. You enthuse about the possibilities of collaboration, demonstrate how it could work, and explain the required next steps.	*e.g. You are responsible for the partnership marketing for your organisation. You identify a new partner with a great fit for one of our leading brands. You present this idea to the lead team.*

Creator **Task:** You are there to...

Check that you can focus on the right thing. The creator prez-type is best when you want to...

...demonstrate »

You **demonstrate** it working... perfectly! You **demo** it successfully accomplishing the very thing it is designed to do. You **demo** it being used by one of them, a layperson.

...enable »

You **enable** the audience to use your creation through explanations. You **enable** them through training. You **enable** them through clear instructional materials.

As you demonstrate your creation to your audience and enable them to use it as you intended, you may consider one or more of the following:

display »

You unveil and exhibit your creation. You make it visible and prominent. You are proud of it and want to make sure your audience can appreciate both its functional attributes and its aesthetic elegance.

explain »

You train them in how it works and what it delivers. You talk through the machinery of it: how each part works in isolation; how each part connects to other parts; how this network of elements comes together to create a practical and useful whole.

instruct »

You instruct them on how to use your creation, to achieve something important for them. You walk them through the steps they can take to make it work for them. You may offer follow-up practical sessions, toolkits, videos, access to further guidance etc.; whatever is necessary so they can correctly utilise your creation.

enthuse »

You excite them in its relevance; its ability to overcome a challenge that they face. You motivate them to use it as you have designed it to be used. You may have evaluated the evidence and shared results, compared with key alternatives, to show the brilliance of this solution. You show pride in what it is and what it can be.

Intensity of Creator

 Mild   Medium   Hot

DRAUGHTSWOMAN   COORDINATOR   BUILDER   **INVENTOR**   DESIGNER   CRAFTSPERSON   **ARTISAN**

Your creator prez-types all have a solution to share, but how much they care about what you do with their design might vary radically.

When your solution is a blueprint, but it is up to your audience to decide how they use it, select a **draughtswoman-creator**. When you have made something to be used as it is designed, select an **inventor-creator**. When it is important to you that your solution is fully utilised and aesthetically admired, select an **artisan-creator**.

Mild-intensity

DRAUGHTS-WOMAN

You have prepared a solution plan, a blueprint, for them to follow. You are confident it will deliver what is needed. You are clear in how it will work for them and will explain to them all and any elements.

The audience now has total freedom in how they choose to use (execute, or apply, or build from) your blueprint in their work.

Medium-intensity

INVENTOR

You have devised an effective and practical solution. You want everyone to use it exactly as designed. You are eager to "lift up the hood" and show the mechanics of how it works. You demonstrate its different uses. You like people to recognise the simple elegance of its final design, but your focus is on its usefulness and efficacy.

The audience is clear on why the solution will deliver against their needs. They have some understanding of its workings. They appreciate the opportunity to road test it with you there to answer questions. They recognise your eagerness for them to use it correctly.

Hot-intensity

ARTISAN

You have toiled long and hard to create a near-perfect solution. It is the seamless blend of function and beauty. You share it proudly. You know it works brilliantly and you are confident that it will be admired and treasured. You believe it would be a worthy winner of an award in design excellence.

Not only are the audience certain that this is the thing to meet their needs, they are also in awe of the elegance of its design.

 # Creator: **Shape Sharpeners**

Tips on how to choose and arrange your content for a creator type of presentation.

Hone Your Messaging

Make your main messages:

solutions

Convince your audience that this creation will solve the problem. Your message should **explain and show how your creation will accomplish the task that is set**.

A method, process, key, remedy, tool, application, instruction, product, recipe, plan.

e.g. *"The Versatile Presenter: Master 12 styles, get the response you need."* Pascoe & Hawkes.

Find ways to ensure they **trust** that the creation works. Perhaps reference the months/years of experimentation that went into creating it; the experts you collaborated with; the excellent product usage test results.

Bring your message, and your creation, to life by making it very **visual** and **repeated**. Keep reminding your audience of a main message. Each time have the creation prominent: the object on the table, a model, a photo, a schematic, or, at the very least, its name and logo.

Shave Your Information

PRIORITISE

The most interesting **features** and most important **benefits**.

☆ **Key components**, especially unique ones, that highlight how it works.

☆ **Evidence** of it achieving the results needed.

INCLUDE

✓ Plans, blueprints, details.

✓ Diagrams and visuals.

✓ Explanation of the key attributes.

✓ Research results.

✓ Demos and case studies.

✓ Testimonials.

✓ Usage instructions.

DEPRIORITISE

The **unnecessary**.

✗ Features that have no benefits.

✗ Unnecessary or abstruse detail.

✗ Discarded prototypes.

✗ Features beyond the need of the audience.

Three Structure – Concept, Model, Application:

A classic way to explain how something works by doing so in three distinct ways.

1) Concept – describe how it works in theory; in abstraction.

2) Model – show it working in the form of a prepared demo or case study.

3) Application – demonstrate it working in a real situation, ideally executed by an exemplar of those who use it in the real world (e.g. a volunteer from the audience).

Time Structure – Usage Instructions:

Unexciting, but effective.

Show the creation working (plan, application, design, etc.) by showing how to use it, step-by-step. To maintain the audience's attention, it is important to first motivate them to want to listen. If the expected benefits are crystal clear, they will listen intently, but if the perceived value is in any way opaque, they may lose focus.

Three Structure – Repeated Wish Fulfilment:

This is a slight evolution of the idea of highlighting features and benefits. In each case, though, you first vocalise the aspiration.

1) Wish – the aspiration that will connect directly to the benefit. It should be an outcome that the audience desires, but in broad terms. This can be a problem solved or a challenge overcome. It can be an aspect of how easy it will be to use. This can be a target number (cost, time, power, etc.).

2) Feature – the component designed into your creation to meet this wish. Keep this short.

3) Benefit – a clear articulation and demonstration of how the feature meets (and maybe exceeds) the wish.

You repeat this trio a number of times, for different benefits. As is often the case, doing it three times may be a perfect balance of depth of information without getting too lengthy.

Great ways to open and close your presentation.

Include in your opening: Let them see the creation; perhaps just a glimpse. Confirm the problem that your creation will solve. Maybe include inferior existing solutions. If true, reference the many hours of intensive work that has gone into designing the creation.

Include in your closing section: Remind them of the many benefits of your creation. Tell them how they get access to it and how they get answers to any questions they have as they start to use it.

 Creator: **Shift Keys**

Signal	Give the creation a name (brand) and primary image (logo). Use this name and image regularly from the start. Show that sufficient time, expertise, and resources have been invested to invent this thing.
Indicate to your audience how to listen.	Have the "creation" there to show the audience (real, model, or blueprint). It may be hidden at first – behind a curtain, ready to be unveiled. Promise a demonstration of it working and that they will get the chance to use it too (either during or after the presentation).

Spoken Language

Language describing why it works can be technical, but keep descriptions of how it works, especially how they will use it, super simple.

Focus on what it does and the results that come from it. Maintain a sense that they will also be able to use it.

Be enthusiastic about all aspects of the creation. The details of how it works and the benefits it brings. But keep some balance; it is "good" or "great", but probably not "the very greatest".

Reference the creation (a lot!). It is the centre of everything. Ideally use a name you have given it.

Emotional language:

○ Convey **joy** in what it does and **anticipation** for what they will be able to achieve from using it.

○ Embody **pride** in the creation itself.

Body Language

Your body language should guide your audience's attention towards the creation. Keep directing their attention to it.

You are likely to use lots of pointing and gesturing. Showing them when to look at the creation as a whole. Indicating when you are focussing on a specific detail.

You want to convey energy and enthusiasm with your body language; don't be still. You are likely to make frequent but brief eye contact with the audience, you want to check they are appropriately analysing and admiring the creation.

Dress in a similar way to the aesthetic of the creation itself – just make sure it looks better than you do. If your creation looks purely functional, then you may choose to look similarly plain. If it looks very technical, you dress like a technician in this field. If it is a finely crafted masterpiece, you look (nearly) as good!

Staging

Your creation takes centre stage so it is clearly the centrepiece.

You should stand to the side of your creation – your gravity is regularly towards your creation.

Consider how you will show many aspects of the creation (through camera, photos, screenshots, etc.). Choreograph moves towards details (close-ups) and moves back to a broader view (wide shots).

You may want to create a space for volunteers to come forward to try out elements of your creation.

 Virtual: Prioritise ways to share the creation, through slides, videos, etc. Can you also share it through your camera (e.g. pack sample, product test, etc.)?

 Small room: Organise chairs in a semi-circle around the creation (on a table or on screen). Have space so you (and any volunteers) can move around the creation.

 Large room: You may need a larger screen than normal for visuals/slides. Can you have a camera to show the creation up close?

Visuals

Your primary visual should be of your creation. If it is an object, it should be on a pedestal with excellent lighting.

If it can only be visualised in 2D (or is too big to bring with you!), the screen and image should be big and clear.

You may share blueprints, sections, organigrams, schematics, photographs, videos etc., anything that lays out the intricacies of your creation.

Your visuals should be accurate, and are also likely to be highly designed and refined, the aesthetics are important.

You primarily use pre-prepared media (e.g. slides; photographs; videos) rather than spontaneous options (e.g. a flip chart). This reinforces that this is a completed thing that will work (if used as recommended).

You may share data charts or videos visualising the excellent results from people using the creation as it was intended to be used.

How To Manage Your Presenter Notes

Ideally, minimise your notes – perhaps just a mind map so you cover the points you have planned. Your creation is your passion – you don't need notes for something that you have spent so much time on.

Where you do choose to consult more detailed notes, use the very instruction materials that you will then pass on to the audience – this way you are enabling them to find this detail themselves after the presentation e.g. bring up the protocol webpage, refer to the FAQs handout, or click into the help box of the application.

Interact

Firstly, you want to demonstrate your creation being used perfectly, perhaps by you, so you allow freedom only to ask questions. Secondly, you want to demonstrate it working well in less experienced hands, perhaps by a volunteer from the audience, so you must offer freedom (with some controls).

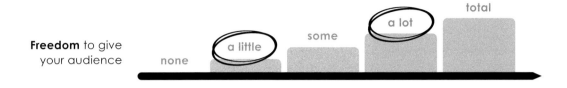

Freedom to give your audience

none · a little · some · a lot · total

You love to get technical questions that give you an opportunity to share more details of its brilliance and clarify how they can all use it correctly.

Therefore:

O Plan sections where your creation is demonstrated to the audience; perhaps by yourself or an expert guest.

O Provide opportunities for the audience to ask questions, seek clarification, confirm understanding etc.

O Give someone from the audience (or a representative) the opportunity to use the creation to complete the task set.

How? *Example processes include:*

O Arrange for a guest to demonstrate – *"Please join me in welcoming Jacob onto the stage. Jacob has agreed to show us how it works."*

O Prepare open questions to ask the audience – *"Can you explain how Lever Y works?"*

O Encourage volunteers up to the front to interact and use the creation – *"Sam, thank you for volunteering to give this a go. Sam – first of all press this button here."*

Ready Yourself

☐ It's absolutely critical that everything will work, so you need to do a full and detailed technical rehearsal. You want to do this in situ, exactly where your presentation is happening, followed by a full dress rehearsal. Have a contingency ready (second prototype, alternative case study) in case your primary plan fails.

☐ If you will ask for a volunteer from the audience, test in advance the demonstration with a few non-experts. Practise your exact instructions; you want to be confident the demonstration will work.

Creator Prez-type **Watch Outs!**

Beware the dark side of the creator prez-type. Avoid:

Rose-tinted Spectacles	Explain Exhaustively
You can be overly convinced in the greatness of your own creation. Nothing is perfect. Try not to be too sensitive to criticism or scepticism.	Avoid being excessively detailed about how it works. Don't forget that others may not need to know the position and orientation of every cog in the mechanism.

Handling likely objections: Help people feel more comfortable in the many details of the creation by taking them through simplified examples and demonstrations. Then give them access to your creation and leave them with a well-indexed instruction manual and specifics on how they contact someone to answer further questions.

Creator Prez-type **Powerful Pairings**

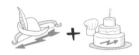

Start as the **maverick** prez-type to shake up the audience's thinking... Things must change ... And we are the ones to do this. Then jump to the **creator** prez-type to show how your plan works.

Embody the **creator** prez-type to explain how your creation solves the challenge, creating a clear understanding of the plan. Then hop into **ruler** prez-type to lay down the law on what steps each person is individually responsible for.

As the **student** prez-type eagerly explain the problem to be solved and your story of how you solved it, including your wrong assumptions and "aha" moments. Then hop to **creator** prez-type to reveal the creation that has risen from your learning experience.

Tricky Transitions: Moving between **creator** prez-type and **hero** prez-type or **lover** prez-type will distract your audience. Your audience must focus on your creation and how it works, therefore they should not be distracted by highlighting the risks of the endeavour (**hero**) or diverted by reminding them of their own perfection (**lover**).

Student

As a **student** prez-type you digest the information to teach the layperson.

Student

As a student-type presenter you study the theories and ideas of others to **create a simplified view of complex things**. You **digest their expertise** and condense everything down to manageable insights.

You are enthusiastic to share your biggest aha moments. You **teach your most practical conclusions**.

The audience appreciates how **you come at the topic from a non-expert's perspective**; you break everything down into easily accessible concepts and ideas.

novice

innocent

amateur

journalist

learner

scholar

connoisseur

The Essence of the Student

From Fiction: In any novel, the reader needs a character who is asking *"what?"*, *"why?"*, and *"who?"* For example, Sherlock Holmes's *"elementary"* deductions would stay mysterious to us without Doctor Watson asking our questions for us. It is Watson's "dumb" questions that keep things simple and clear for us, the reader.

In many stories, it is the hero themself, who has been thrown into unfamiliar surroundings, who asks all the questions for us. Percy Jackson in Rick Riordan's excellent adventures does exactly this.

In some stories there is a more innocent type of student; they ask questions that seem naïve at first, with answers that become vital in time e.g. Dory from *Finding Nemo* and Luna Lovegood from the Harry Potter books.

From Real World: In the excellent TED Talk *Your Elusive Creative Genius*, Elizabeth Gilbert muses on the unrealistic expectations laid on artists to be geniuses.[33] She sparkles as she reveals key insights that she has come to understand through her interactions with greater minds than hers. She shares her perspectives but at no point purports to be the expert with a definitive correct answer. In fact, she actively downplays her own know-how, imploring the audience to see her as the same as any of them.

TV and streaming docuseries and magazine shows often have a presenter in a student style. For example, the *Fully Charged* YouTube channel ran a series on buying a first electric car.[34] The presenter is Maddie, who knows little more than we do, talks to lots of experts, and then shares how she squares all the expert advice with her own real-world experience. Google "Fully Charged Maddie Goes Electric" to watch.

Being your student prez-type enables you to **convey knowledge** without being, or pretending to be, an expert in the topic. You have worked hard to break down all the complexity into something anyone from the audience can comprehend. You **teach what you have learnt**, NOT to be all knowing in all things related to the topic. This can be liberating.

 Student: **When to Select**

Choose to be a student prez-type when you need a way to strip away any perceived complexity to present knowledge that feels simple and accessible to all in the audience.

Select the student prez-type when you want to...

...help your audience learn something.	You have something to teach your audience. You share models, principles, best practices, facts and figures, and more. Throughout you focus on accessible ways to understand each element and the whole: metaphors, diagrams, shorthands, etc.	*e.g. You want your team to learn about the valuable work of a local charity that you are collaborating with.*
...provide rationale to support a point of view, without time to get into detail.	You have a conclusion, or recommendation, to put across. You share this as an output of your "studies". Your hard work means others need not analyse everything themselves. They know you are not lost in the academic details, and they trust that you will concentrate on ideas that have relevance within the real world they work in.	*e.g. You need sign-off from leadership on where to hold the quarterly team meeting. They only need to know enough to say yes to a non-contentious question.*
...summarise a broader and deeper set of content.	You want to provide an overview of your topic. You find intuitive and visual ways to lay out and connect the ideas in short form. You find core messages (mantras, principles, tips, conclusions) that tie together the knowledge into practical ideas.	*e.g. You want to summarise the conclusions of a meta-analysis on shopping habit changes across convenience stores.*
...share expertise when you are not the expert.	You embrace your relative inexperience and take on the role of an eager and curious pupil. You enjoy each fresh idea, fact, and figure that you grasp. You introduce the expertise of others (e.g. quotes). You are eager to hear from "true experts" in the room, but focus on ensuring other non-experts understand things well enough for them.	*e.g. You want to share the most interesting info from a recent book on current uses of AI. This will enable a broad open discussion on potential uses for the business.*

Student **Task:** You are there to...

Check that you can focus on the right thing. The student prez-type is best when you want to...

...digest »

You **digest** the array of possible sources down to a few. You **digest** the information down to simple ideas. You **digest** the expert's interpretations into basic insights.

...teach »

You **teach** the insights that you have formed. You **teach** where you found it and why you trust it. You **teach** how they might use it.

As you digest information and teach the content, concentrate on one or more of the following:

summarise »

You pull out the main points and the most important supporting headlines from your content. Details may be shared for interest, but what matters is a broad understanding of key facts and ideas.

translate »

You translate the complex information into forms that this audience will understand. Clarify all technical terminology, rephrasing everything into common language. You will connect all concepts that seem alien to this audience to terms and models that they are familiar with.

codify »

You capture the digested information into a format that can be consistently and reliably utilised. You turn complex analysis into manageable formulas. You will find creative ways to systemise complex information in a way the audience will understand.

broadcast »

You communicate your simple ideas out to a broad audience. You work to make the information accessible to as many in the audience as you can. You highlight the central insights in each story.

Intensity of Student

 Mild   Medium   Hot

NOVICE   INNOCENT   AMATEUR   **JOURNALIST**   LEARNER   SCHOLAR   **CONNOISSEUR**

As a student prez-type you may know next to nothing or you may, actually, know quite a lot.

When you are truly new to a topic, select a **novice-student**. When you have a fair understanding of the topic you may want to aim right into the middle of this prez-type and select a **journalist-student**. When the audience already sees you as an expert, switch on your **connoisseur-student**, where you are the expert in other peoples' expertise.

Mild-intensity

NOVICE

You have no direct experience in the topic. You knew nothing until very recently. This gives you an eagerness and an openness to learn. You will eagerly ask the most basic of questions with no fear of embarrassment. You will introduce the trusted "teachers" who teach you so much. You are grateful for all the time they have spent explaining and clarifying ideas for you.

Your audience can relax as you ask all the fundamental questions and lay out, in the most basic way, the most relevant information.

Medium-intensity

JOURNALIST

You represent the layperson determined to learn all that is pertinent from those with direct expertise. Even if you have some grounding in the topic, or even significant experience, you focus on asking important questions and forming digestible explanations. You source questions from the audience as well as ask those that seem relevant to you.

Your audience watches and learns as you ask gently probing questions whenever anything is unclear.

Hot-intensity

CONNOISSEUR

You are the expert in other peoples' expertise. You are fascinated by the greatest experts in your specific field of interest. You avidly mine all the knowledge that you can from these subject specialists. acquire a truly impressive range of insights and best examples through your study.

Your audience may see you as an expert yourself, but you know you are not. This will allow you to be a simplifying bridge between the true experts and the audience.

Student: **Shape Sharpeners**

Tips on how to choose and arrange your content for a student type of presentation.

Hone Your Messaging

Make your main messages:

learnings

You want to lead with a message that **summarises some way of understanding** the knowledge that you are sharing.

An insight, "aha", adage, principle, formula, tip.

e.g. "*An apple a day keeps the doctor away.*"
English proverb.

Keep to **simple** words and concepts widely known and understood by your audience. Look to connect to things that already feel simple: analogies, metaphors and similes.

Ensure your message is easily seen as **trustworthy**. Reinforce your message by connecting it to a credible and established source. This might be a known topic expert or a convincing data set.

Shave Your Information

PRIORITISE

Simple to understand and easy to **trust**.

☆ **Simple visuals:** basic diagrams, concepts distilled into visual summaries, simple charts, videos, etc.

☆ Information from a **known source**. Their data, or data they use often. Info and ideas that connect to or build from models/processes they are familiar with.

INCLUDE

✓ Well established ideas and insights: methods, formula, best practice, etc.

✓ Analogies and metaphors rooted in well-understood concepts to explain harder to grasp concepts.

✓ Example stories of how the insights relate to everyday experiences – yours and/or your audience's.

✓ Stories of your learning through mistakes.

DEPRIORITISE

The **confusing**.

✗ Things you do not understand.

✗ Deeper explanation beyond what is needed.

✗ Contradictory information.

✗ Unnecessary areas of debate or differing expert opinions.

Great ways to structure parts of your presentation.

Two Structure – Straight Comparison:

Group content into two separate and distinct areas. Things often feel simpler when you make comparisons. Options include:

O Compare your content with a model they already know well.

O Look at the topic from two separate perspectives (e.g. retailer vs shopper).

O Compare with a known case study.

One Structure – Easy Metaphor:

Connect the complex ideas that seem confusingly complex to a metaphorical idea that we easily understand. Connect each element of the information you share to an aspect of the consistent metaphor. As you build up a picture of these thinking connections, you build up their comprehension of the complex idea.

Story Structure – Newspaper Story:

Use a classic journalistic story structure:

1) Introduce to the audience someone struggling with a challenge.

2) Link their story to your broader topic, and quote insights from subject experts/data.

3) Analyse and contextualise the facts against this broad insight.

4) Return to how it affects our "someone" from the beginning.

Great ways to open and close your presentation.

Include in your opening: Lay out the questions that you have/had looking into the topic. Check the audience's present level of understanding. Promise to share how you got to your "aha!" moments as well as the information itself.

Tell the audience where your information comes from e.g. teacher, expert, author, data source. Spend time explaining why these sources are eminent and expert in the topic. Introduce your overview of what you have learned and will share.

Include in your closing section: Recap main ideas shared, leaving them with a summary of just a few key points. Perhaps only include a single overall insight.

Student: **Shift Keys**

Signal

Indicate to your audience how to listen.

Make it clear that you are acting as a non-expert layperson (even if you are actually an expert). Show humility – share your uncertainty in whether you were capable of understanding the complex ideas.

Introduce who you have learned from, in a way that shows your high regard for their expertise and your appreciation for them taking the time to teach you. Give the audience a sense of the time and energy you have invested to learn from others.

Spoken Language

Use language that can be easily understood by your audience. It's important to you that everyone understands what you are telling them.

Clarify any technical vocabulary that you need to use that might not be understood by your audience.

Frame questions you are looking to answer.

Stay modest/humble about your intelligence; you are not trying to impress your audience regarding your own abilities.

Emotional language:

○ Talk of your **curiosity** and **anticipation** to learn.

○ Confess to your **joy** as you learn.

○ Talk of your **admiration** for those who you learn from.

Body Language

Keep stance and gestures open – accepting everyone into the ideas that you are sharing.

Keep gestures most energised when sharing your "eureka" moments of understanding.

Stay attentive to your audience; you are keen to catch audience questions and check understanding. Tip: regularly set your feet so they point out towards your audience.

Guide (arm movement) the audience's attention towards the ideas and information that you are sharing.

Dress similarly to your audience (e.g. lab coat if they are in lab coats). No need to dress to impress (e.g. everyday suit, not best suit).

Staging

Position yourself to one side of your "stage". Centre stage is for the knowledge you share (display) and the teachers you learnt from. Ideally you are at the same level as your audience (e.g. you and they are sat).

Position the audience so they all feel equally able to ask questions. Give them space to feel comfortable but close to others to discuss ideas that come up.

Can you create distinct areas for the complex information from the experts and your simplified interpretations and insights?

 Virtual: Compliment the use of formal slides with other options (e.g. thoughts on a digital whiteboard, a model on a second webcam, a scan of sketched notes).

 Small room: If expert content is shared from the central screen, your simple explanations are best positioned to the side (or on the table in the middle).

 Large room: Choreograph so you can move forward from where you share information to where your audience is sat.

Visuals

Show the experts (books, photo of teacher, research paper) that are your sources. Represent their credibility (CV, academic role, book sales, etc.).

Bring your teacher(s) into the room: photo, quotes, references, videos, etc.

Reduce the number of visuals/slides to only those needed to teach your insights. Keep it simple.

Turn your insight summary into a basic drawing – a rough sketch, a basic diagram. Content originally from your teacher can look complex but your summary should look simple.

Basic tools are ideal as you explain how you have digested and summarised the complex ideas. Use a flip chart, whiteboard, photo of your sketch on paper, simple slide, main insights pinned onto a board, etc.

Have a simple summary (e.g. a one-pager) to hand out afterwards.

How To Manage Your Presenter Notes

Elements of your talk may be scripted (e.g. quotes, definitions, etc.), but don't script everything (if possible). Have sketched notes of your full talk, so you can look down at any moment to see where you are. If needed, have more detailed notes only for moments where you need them most.

Where your presentation builds on the expert content of others, have the sources to hand. The book you have read, with key sections marked for you to go to if needed. The link to their online biography to read out as you introduce a specialist. The market report loaded onto your e-reader with sections highlighted.

Interact

Aim to keep a good level of control. You want to keep discussions safely on topic and you want to avoid broad debate. That stated, you do want to hear questions so you can help people understand important ideas.

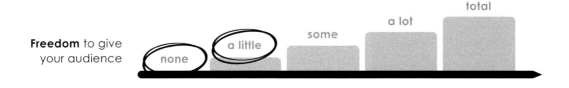

Freedom to give your audience: none, a little, some, a lot, total

Therefore:

O Plan ways to regularly check for their questions and understanding.

O Be open to questions from the audience, but withhold the right to park any for after the presentation (perhaps directed to someone more expert than you).

How? *Example processes include:*

O Surveys with closed questions – *"Hands up if anything so far is unclear."*

O Interview a pre-arranged guest – *"Professor, thank you for joining us today. Let me start by asking you…"*

O Audience Q&A with a pre-arranged guest – *"Who has the first question to ask the professor?"*

Ready Yourself

☐ Practise, practise, practise. You do not know content well enough to "wing it".

☐ Remind yourself of questions you originally had and your excitement in finding answers.

☐ Think through potential questions you may get and how you will answer (or park) them.

☐ If feeling nervous, warm-up to release anxiety: stretch jaw, shoulders, leg muscles.

Student Prez-type **Watch Outs!**

Beware the dark side of the student prez-type. Avoid:

Naively Uncredible

You can be easily dismissed as non-expert. Establish the credibility of your sources so others see the value in what you are sharing.

Surface Scratcher

Avoid delivering an overly simplistic summary of the situation; acknowledge if the topic is complicated and nuanced.

Handling likely objections: Don't feel the need to know the answers to all questions; however, be ready to signpost relevant sources/references/experts. The student prez-type has the advantage of being open to admit their limitations, and learn more, perhaps from experts in your audience.

Student Prez-type **Powerful Pairings**

You predominantly embody the **student** prez-type, carefully setting the credibility of the experts that you have learnt from. Jumping periodically in and out of the **jester** prez-type can entertain and re-engage your audience.

Begin as a **sage** prez-type, confident in your existing knowledge and expertise. Come to an area that you do not understand, and hop into **student** prez-type, eager to learn from others.

Start as the **student** prez-type, laying out the published knowledge in an area of interest, open to and impressed by the experts' wisdom. At a key point you start to question the established "facts" and jump into the **maverick** prez-type, challenging the status quo.

Tricky Transitions: Moving between **student** prez-type and **everyman** prez-type or **magician** prez-type can feel uneasy to your audience. You are promising that something not well known can be better understood, which is inconsistent with traditions known by everyone (**everyman**) or power that no one fully comprehends (**magician**).

4

GOING
FURTHER

Here, in Part 4: GOING FURTHER, we propel you further and faster as you use **The Prez Method**. You will read:

☆ Star Tips ☆

Look up to the night sky to discover ancient wisdoms. Practical advice for each of the four steps of Set, Select, Sharpen, and Shift.

△ Change Tips △

Combine and move between prez-types. Sensible ways to sail between prez-types during a presentation. Which transitions are easiest, which are most dramatic, and which include dangerous waters that can scuttle an unwary ship.

Uniquely Yours

Personalise a prez-type so it feels true to you. More thoughts on how you may mix the essential elements of any prez-type with all that is great about you.

Finally, we explain more about the origins of prez-types.

A Little More On Archetypes

Learning from psychology, marketing theory, and drama. For those keen to delve a little deeper.

Firstly, we share some general 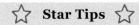 **Star Tips**.

☆ Star **Tips** ☆

Gaze up into the star-filled night sky. There is ancient wisdom to be found.

We have been working with **The Prez Method** for many years. We have accumulated many ☆ tips (star tips) along the way. Sometimes from eureka moments we found in neighbouring disciplines, sometimes by trial and error, and sometimes by fortunate accident. We offer you a small constellation of our favourites, set out by the four steps of **The Prez Method**.

The greatest challenge we face can be the limitation to set only one direction of prez-intent. We often have many things we want to achieve. Can we break from the shackles of a single prez-intent? The next chapter, '△ Change Tips △ ', gets into this question. It includes tips on how to combine different prez-types to achieve more than one prez-intent.

For now, we offer a single ☆ tip for **SET your prez-intent: What is Holding Them Back?**

☆ TIP	SET	What is Holding Them Back?	Write down what you want your audience to do (or feel). Then ask yourself what is preventing them from doing it (or feeling it).

This flip in perspective, from what you want them to do, to what is stopping them doing it, can help you get to the nub of the matter. Write down what you want your audience to do as a result of your presentation. Then consider the question: what is the biggest obstacle to them doing this today?

This question helps clarify whether the priority is to fill a knowledge gap, change their thinking, build trust, or clarify next steps. You will likely be tempted to include all four, but which one will have the greatest impact? Prioritise that direction.

We move our attention to the next group of ☆ tips...

We often come across a presenter who knows which prez-type they <u>should</u> select, but for a variety of reasons they hesitate to do so. They stare at the arrow that they marked as their prez-intent, see the bearing points directly to a particular prez-type that makes a completely logical choice, and yet they feel uncomfortable selecting it.

> For example, Team Leader Emma needs to direct her team to complete their personal development plans for the next twelve months, laying out where they will invest time (and Emma's budget) in training and coaching. The directive has come down from the general manager that all plans must be completed, signed off by Emma, and uploaded onto the system by the end of the week. She knows it makes sense to select the ruler prez-type, but Emma has always prided herself on embodying servant leadership. She actively avoids "bossing people around". But still … ruler prez-type would be the ideal style to embody. How do we help Emma?

We offer two ☆ tips for **SELECT your prez-type: Have Faith, But Practise Safe** and **Aim for a More Mellow Flavour.**

SELECT
☆ **TIP 1**

Have Faith, But Practise Safe

You are capable of embodying each and every prez-type, so trust yourself. But pick sensible situations to test pilot a prez-type for the first time.

The prez-types each codify a part of the human existence. That sounds rather grand, but it is true. Through our lives we learn, create, direct, care, collaborate, love, laugh, challenge the status quo, harness powerful tools, take on noble causes, explore, and share wisdom. We may do a lot of some and far less of others, but they are all things we do during our time on this planet. By the time you are an adult you have experience in each and every one of the twelve prez-types.

However, if a prez-type feels a little alien to you, it is good to give it a trial run in a safe space. Look for situations where you can take a few performance risks. Maybe plan more rehearsal time and invite a friend to observe – get their feedback as you take tentative steps with the prez-type. Maybe run a test flight of a prez-type at a family event where the worst outcome, if it goes badly, is gentle mockery from your sibling. Create safe ways to give things a go.

The first time you try a prez-type does not have to be in front of an important audience.

SELECT
☆ TIP 2

Aim for a More Mellow Flavour

Start in a lower-intensity level of the prez-type. Every prez-type has different sub-types. Pick one that feels less spicy.

Each prez-type offers a smorgasbord of tastes and textures. However, if a cuisine is new to you or you know it is a little spicy for your liking, it is OK to aim for the more mellow flavours. If you do not feel ready to bite into the fieriest peppers, start with the lower-intensity options for that prez-type.

Here are three examples to consider:

As the **jester prez-type** you do not need to be inherently hilarious, you may only want to be playful.

Go to "Intensity of Jester" page within the DO IT: Jester chapter and you will find you have many intensities of **jester** to choose from. Aim for a milder version. Perhaps choose to play the **fool-jester:**

Lean into being a little ridiculous and silly, but do not push any further. In any situation, there is a form of irreverent behaviour that is still appropriate and respectful.

As the **fool-jester** there is no pressure to be funny, just the freedom to be foolish.

As the **explorer prez-type** you do not need to be obsessively pioneering, you may only want to be softly curious.

Go to "Intensity of Explorer" page within the DO IT: Explorer chapter. Stay safe by embracing the **scout-explorer:**

Plan to travel shorter distances across your content while staying inquisitive. Let yourself go down a few side paths; feel excited as you step into a neighbouring topic; take a few tentative steps into new territories; but never venture too far away from base camp.

This is still being an **explorer prez-type** – just a low-intensity version.

As the **ruler prez-type** you do not need to be dictatorial, you may only want to be firm.

Go to the "Intensity of Ruler" page within the DO IT: Ruler chapter. Focus on being the **gatekeeper-ruler:**

Stand tall and stay strong, but do not pretend to be anyone's superior. Instead, focus on how, for your audience to accomplish something desirable, they first need to complete a sequence of unambiguous steps. These steps have been commanded by a higher authority (who they are most welcome to visit and challenge). There is no debate, and there are no alternatives; they simply need to do as you tell them. Once done, they can proceed with their day.

This is still a great **ruler** option, but does not rely on you holding some high authority.

For each prez-type there are multiple alternatives. The sixth page of each DO IT chapter includes a variety of options for that prez-type. For example:

Mild	Medium	Hot
ADVOCATE BUDDY SIDEKICK	**CHEERLEADER**	ENDORSER ADMIRER **#1 FAN**

You may struggle with the thought of being a **lover prez-type**, but feel at ease being an "admirer". If the role of "admirer" resonates, take that as the word that helps you sharpen your presentation and shift your delivery. Or you might prefer "sidekick" or "endorser". Select whichever feels best for you.

Gavin's Story: I Don't Feel I Can Challenge Them, But...

In 2019, Gavin was booked to deliver a market trends presentation at a conference in Romania. He was an experienced and capable presenter. He was an expert in the grocery industry in the UK. The conference was for those across the retail industry in countries including Romania, Poland and Hungary. Gavin was briefed to bring a new perspective on how grocery retail could be done in the region.

When Gavin analysed the objectives of the presentation, he felt his prez-intent was halfway between **Change** and **Belonging**. His task was to build rapport with an audience who did not know him and to propose that the industry would have to evolve in the coming years. The prez-intent pointed directly to the **maverick prez-type**.

However, Gavin felt he had a problem. He did not feel he had the right to challenge the way food retail was done in Eastern Europe. He did not have the depth of background. His expertise was in the UK. Also, **maverick** felt like an uncomfortable fit. His natural style was to be collaborative and kind, not to throw opinions out like hand grenades. Presenting to a new audience in a new setting, he needed a prez-type that he felt confident in.

Gavin trusted **The Prez Method**, so looked into the intensity options for **maverick**.

Mild	Medium	Hot
OUTSIDER PROVOCATEUR CHALLENGER	**REFORMER**	PROGRESSIVE REBEL **REVOLUTIONARY**

He quickly realised that he could imagine being the **outsider-maverick** – to cover content with a vantage point at a distance from those in the audience. He saw that this perfectly matched his role at the conference. He was booked to provide an outsider's perspective. He would question elements of the retail industry that confused him, that seemed contrary to what worked in markets like the UK. He would not push a particular point of view, but he would draw attention to the fact an alternative view existed.

Gavin had moved from feeling like **maverick prez-type** was never going to be a viable selection to feeling inspired and enthusiastic to be an **outsider-maverick**.

The Versatile Presenter

☆ ☆ TIPS  3 SHARPEN YOUR PREZ-CONTENT

Next we look at ☆ tips related to SHARPEN. There are lots of hints we want to give you as you design your presentation to match your chosen prez-type. We constrain ourselves to two. The first tip is an idea as old as storytelling. The second tip is shiny and new.

SHARPEN ☆ TIP 1 | **Embrace Crafting Constraints** | The secret to designing a great presentation can be to consciously limit yourself. Strategic restrictions give you focus and encourage creativity.

Leonardo da Vinci once said:

> *"Art lives from constraints and dies from freedom."*

Lots of art comes out of the restrictions that exist: the tightness of the budget, the limit of available time, the shortage of resources, the compact nature of the canvas, the whims of the powerful, the desires of the paying public. The list goes on. Each of these factors constrains the creator, but they also focus their mind on the space they get to be creative in.

As you prepare your presentation, go to the first page of the **Shape Sharpeners** section (within your prez-type chapter). Consider the ideas you find there as design restrictions. Not as guidance to consider; nor as a suggestion to ignore; nor as "thought starters". Use them as constraints!

For example, if you select the **magician prez-type**, you work your way through its **Shape Sharpener** page.

1) You take a piece of paper, write "**a vision**" at the top, and force yourself to form your message as a vision (or a prophecy, promise, miracle, dream, capability, or a power).

2) You review the content that you could include and make yourself remove most, if not all, of the content that can be described as: "**The how: technical explanations.**"

3) You review the content that you could include and prioritise "Things that have **impact** and are **spectacular**."

This may feel uncomfortable, but the constraint will enable you to edit well, and then it will release you to be creative.

Next we look at a modern idea: how to combine the tips and ideas in this book with a Generative AI tool.

SHARPEN ☆ TIP 2 | **Use GenAI to Generate a Sketch** | Use the SHARPEN prompts within the relevant prez-type chapter to instruct a Generative AI tool to write a draft text for you to build from.

As we write this book in 2024, Generative AI large language models (LLMs) are exploding into our working lives.[35] ChatGPT is the tool that broke into the public's consciousness. Gemini, Microsoft Co-Pilot, and Apple Intelligence are all in various stages of development. As you read this book, new LLM names may already feel ubiquitous. Perhaps you have an Apple Intelligence chip installed into your prefrontal lobe, offering up AI generated language for you to pick from as you write your next email on your iPhone?

Whichever tool you use, LLMs are great thought starters for how you might write and structure your presentation. They may not (yet) be good enough to provide your exact script, but they are a great means to get you started. They are brilliant at writing in different styles. If you give the tool a few directing instructions, it is amazing what it will come up with.

This is another way that this book becomes invaluable. The DO IT chapters give you perfect prompts to direct a Generative AI tool. Without these prompts the LLM has little way of forming the right style of presentation. With these prompts, you have the guiding instructions <u>and</u> the tool to create options.

Example Story: Richard Uses Generative AI to Sharpen His Heroic Presentation

I dived into ChatGPT and typed out the following:

"I want to introduce Jane to my team. Write me a short five-minute presentation script. Facts include: Jane is joining to review and renew our invoicing processes; recent audit brought up issues with invoicing that we need to fix; if we fail to fix them jobs will be lost; Jane has fifteen years of experience fixing issues like this; don't worry, we have this. Write the presentation in the style of a hero archetype: set out a vital cause that we must take on. Highlight the dangers of not taking any action. Inspire people to feel ready to roll up their sleeves and get going."

Perhaps inevitably, the tool got overly creative. Its first attempt included:

"Today, we stand at the precipice of destiny, where the clarion call of duty echoes through the halls of our domain. For we face a perilous foe, a shadow lurking in the depths of our invoicing abyss, threatening the very fabric of our noble enterprise."

Hmmm… This is many steps too evocative for a real-world business presentation. So I asked the tool to rewrite the presentation and to "*tone it down*". The tool duly obliged, and now the opening was:

> "*Today, we find ourselves at a pivotal moment in our journey, facing a challenge that requires our collective attention and resolve. It is with a sense of purpose that I introduce Jane to our team.*"

This still needs finessing, but it feels close to something that I could stand and say to a business team. And it sets the right tone for the important messages I have planned. I can pull out key phrases and work them into language that fits my style and the details I need to get across. I might end up with something like:

> "*Team, we find ourselves at a pivotal moment in the work we do. The truth is we are facing a challenge that requires our collective attention and significant resolve. We must fix our invoicing processes in time for the next audit – failing to do so would lead to lost jobs.*

> "*This morning I am here to introduce you all to Jane, our new finance leader. It is always a joy to bring someone of Jane's calibre and character into our team, but today I need you all to focus on why Jane is joining us … I need you in no doubt: it is vital that we fix the issues to get our invoicing protocols back on track.*"

By starting with the LLM version I have quickly come to a language that fits me and what I want to achieve.

Not only can you ask a GenAI tool for starting language, you can ask it to arrange your points in specific structures. If you like a particular structure idea within the prez-type chapter, use this to instruct the GenAI tool how to organise the information. It will do this quickly and effectively.

GenAI tools can also create presentation decks for you. Prezi and Gamma (and many others) offer presentation deck creating tools driven (and edited) using AI. Again, use the prompts in this book to better guide the GenAI tool.

You will still have a lot of work to do, but using a GenAI tool can be helpful. Your work becomes more about tailoring what the GenAI tool has created to the needs you have for the specific presentation.

It is time to move onto our final set of ☆ tips: the largest constellation. It will guide your way as you SHIFT into each prez-type.

In the really-really of working life, how do I shift my style of delivery?

For many of the people that we work with, this is the biggest question they have with implementing **The Prez Method**.

Trust us, everyone can survive and thrive embodying any of the twelve prez-types. We admit, however, that there are challenges. Below we offer three helpful ☆ tips relating to SHIFT.

☆ TIP **SHIFT** ☆ **TIP 1**   **Nudge Cues**   Place a visual reminder of your chosen prez-type in your eyeline. Each time it catches your eye you will be subtly prompted.

We all need a gentle nudge from time to time. Presenting is no different. In fact, it is a time when the nudge becomes more important. Even if you start your presentation in the planned style, you have so many things to think about as you talk through your content, it is natural to slide back to your habitual presenting style. You **regress back to routine**.

What works is to form a small visual reminder and place it where you will regularly see it as you present. Let's say you have selected magician prez-type. You may:

O Draw a magician's hat in neon green pen in the corner of each of your notes cards. As you look at each card you are nudged back to embody the magician.

O Type "*You are a magician*" in your speaker notes for each slide. As you review the notes, you are nudged.

O Ask a colleague to give you a signal, perhaps a magical twirl of a finger, each time the magician fades from your delivery. Each twirl gives you a nudge.

O Bring a card with the magician prez-type image on it and place this on the table by your notes. As you glance down you see it and you are nudged.

Whenever you see this nudge cue you are reminded to shift back into your presenting style.

You may worry that the audience could notice your nudge cue. Would this undermine what you are doing? In reality, you will find that the audience rarely notices. They are focussed on what you are saying and showing them on your slides – they don't worry about little reminders you have. On those rare occasions when they do spot your nudge cue, you explain to them that it is a reminder to you on how you want to speak. In our experience, they thank you warmly for the genius tip and ask where they can find out more (we recommend you show them this book).

SHIFT
☆ TIP 2

Switch from "Be" to "Do"

If you are struggling to "be" the prez-type, switch to "do" the prez-type.

The fourth step of **The Prez Method** asks you to bring to mind your prez-type, and use this to inspire your use of language, body language and more. This prez-type is a type of character to embody – a version of you to "be".

Occasionally, we come across people who find it tricky to "be" a prez-type. It feels uneasy or counterproductive. They are often experienced, smart people who are highly effective presenters. They just find it tricky to "be" the prez-type.

We have found that these people are much more comfortable to "do" the prez-type. They use the prez-type as a shortcut to a task to focus on as they present. They are "do" presenters rather than "be" presenters.

For "do" presenters, rather than choosing to embody ("be") a prez-type and saying something like *I am a hero* they prefer to lean into a **heroic-type task** ("do") such as *I am here to convince them*". This short articulation of an action or task helps this presenter shift how they present.

They still benefit from consciously crafting the presentation using the language of the hero prez-type. But once they move to deliver the presentation, they **focus on what they are doing rather than what they are being**.

If this works best for you, that is great. You will find in the DO IT chapters a "[Prez-type] Task: You are there to…" This will always have **two primary task words** (e.g. for hero: "*convince* ≫" and "*inspire* ≫") and **four secondary task words** (e.g. for hero: "*strive* ≫", "*risk* ≫", "*believe* ≫", and "*manoeuvre* ≫"). Look out for the ≫ after each task word; one of these words might be an ideal choice for you to focus on.

Choosing to "do" the prez-type is a very effective, powerful, way to shift your presentation delivery style. If you drive your delivery behind a task to focus on, your audience intuitively picks up on it. If this is your preferred route, to concentrate on "do" rather than "be", it is a great route to take.

Two SHIFT ☆ tips covered. We move our gaze towards the final ☆ tip in this constellation…

SHIFT
☆ **TIP 3**

Concede to Succeed

Relinquish control and let your instincts take over. Surrender to the prez-type and your authentic prez-style will shine through.

This tip reads like a self-help trope. An idea found in a well-meaning book on how to "live your best life". Does this really fit in a practical book about presentation skills? Don't dismiss this ☆ tip just yet! There is a valuable point here.

If you know any principles of behavioural psychology you may be well versed in the concept of "System 1 and System 2" (or sometimes described as "Brain 1 and Brain 2").[36] "System 1" is your subconscious brain, which thinks intuitively and instinctively. "System 2" is your conscious brain, which considers information deeply and thinks through things before coming to a response.

"Concede to Succeed" is encouraging you to push your conscious, intellectual brain (System 2) out of the way. To stop your conscious brain interfering and to let your instinctive subconscious brain (System 1) do what it does best. You want to quieten your analytical thinking to allow your innate thinking to drive your presentation delivery.

In order to do this, you need to concede control to your subconscious. To put this in a less grand way: stop overthinking it and just do it! For example, as you present, don't worry about what a sage would do, just be a sage!

You may feel that this is "*easier said than done*". You struggle to imagine how this might be practical when you have thirty minutes to complete your presentation, twenty slides to work through, ten pairs of eyes staring at you, and one objective (prez-intent) to achieve. Trust us. It will help. We admit it takes some practice.

The inspiration for this ☆ tip is from the acting world. Actors have pages of dialogue to recite, stage moves to perfect, props to pick up, costume changes to undertake, etc. Their challenge is the same as your challenge: to complete all these activities while putting across a truthful and engaging performance. Actors learn to surrender to the role – to let their intuitive-self take more control.[37] They do not surrender completely – their conscious brain is still checking that they correctly complete the mechanics of the scene – but they rely more on the intuitive responses to put across meaning.

You do the same. Practise turning down your conscious brain (that interferes) and turning up your instinctive brain. Let go a little. Learn from actors. Surrender to the prez-type.

That completes our journey through the ☆ tips. We bring our attention to how we might travel between prez-types in the same presentation.

△ Change **Tips** △

Combining and moving between prez-types.

When we first explained **The Prez Method** (in Part 2: The PREZ METHOD), we encouraged you to keep things simple: to put down anchor at just one prez-type. This was wise advice. However, in reality, **many of the most important presentations that you deliver as a business leader will involve moving between a small number of different prez-types.**

You may start the presentation as a **maverick prez-type**, then consciously jump over to be a **creator prez-type**, before skipping across to be a **caregiver prez-type**. This is not as easy as staying as one prez-type throughout, but as we shall see, there are many advantages in doing so.

In this chapter we look into the value of transitioning between prez-types. We explain when to plan to change prez-type. We give you a range of △ tips (change tips) on how to do it well.

When to Change **Prez-types**

CHANGE
△ TIP 1

Choose Not To

There is great benefit in sticking to one prez-type for any one presentation. Presenting is hard enough already!

Staying within one prez-type feels consistent to your audience. If I go to a music concert, I expect one style of music. An evening of classical music, <u>or</u> songs from a favourite band, <u>or</u> a mix of jazz pieces. If the musicians played a Mozart violin concerto, then screamed an Iron Maiden cover, before tripping through a Nina Simone jazz standard, I would be impressed, but perhaps a little confused, and I am not sure I would be very happy.

Stick to one prez-type if you can. However, you might choose to challenge yourself to travel between multiple prez-types because...

CHANGE
△ TIP 2

Variety is the Spice of Life

Your audience is energised by variation. They don't want chaos, but they do want well-structured variety.

As we grow our skills in anything, what seemed dumbfoundingly difficult before starts to feel manageable. In inexperienced hands, complexity can bring unwelcome noise, but in skilled hands the same complexity can bring nuance and flair. By combining prez-types you can navigate more complicated journeys.

The more complete presenter learns to dextrously add complexity and prepare a presentation with multiple prez-types. Here are five good reasons why you might select more than one prez-type:

1) **To double-down**. You have only one prez-intent, one direction, but instead of picking one prez-type from this bearing, you pick two. The audience stays in one form of listening, but you add variety and emphasis.

   E.g. You want to inspire your audience to see a problem differently (prez-intent = change). You decide to use **hero** prez-type followed by **magician** prez-type. The former calls everyone to "act now or repent at leisure" then the latter wows them with the amazing results of the pilot.

The Versatile Presenter

2) **To double-up**. Sometimes, as a leader, you really do have more than one outcome you need to achieve from your presentation. You only have one meeting to deliver the message, one throw of the dice. You have to work towards both objectives.

> E.g. You are presenting the end-of-quarter business review to the team. You would prefer to focus only on confidence and team spirit (prez-intent = belonging) as there has been lots of churn in personnel, with many being new to the team. However, there is a directive from the global head office to get everyone to train on the latest corporate confidentiality policies. You don't want to muddy one message with the other, and you do not have the time to split into two separate presentations. So you plan to do some of the presentation as **lover** prez-type then move to **ruler** prez-type.

3) **To refresh attention**. Listening hard can become tiring for the audience. The audience benefits from occasional mental breaks. A "cognitive palate-cleanser". You give them a respite from thinking one way by encouraging them to use their brain in a very different way. This can refresh their focus and engagement.

> E.g. You are deploying a major new initiative. Your objective is to teach the audience a significant amount of important information about why the initiative exists and why it will work (prez-intent = knowledge). You decide to present mostly in a **sage** prez-type: to help the audience understand the information. You plan intermittent jumps into being a **jester** prez-type: these short moments of fun will refresh their energy.

4) **To mark transitions**. For a longer presentation, you may use a change of prez-type to help bridge sections. Often this is moving from an opening section into a section of content, or moving from covering a topic into a broader analysis.

> E.g. You are delivering a ninety-minute presentation as part of a major review to the lead team. You choose to open as an **everyman** prez-type, to build rapport with the audience. You switch into an **explorer** prez-type as you cover the central content. You make a second shift into the **caregiver** prez-type to guide them on what to do next.

5) **When needs must**. There will be times when your carefully formed plan falls apart; when the prez-type you selected fails "to cut the mustard". The audience is not where you thought they were, so you need to change tack, and fast. Your objective needs to fundamentally alter based on new information. In these situations, you take a moment to reassess and then nimbly switch into a new prez-type. These are some of the most exhilarating presentation moments.

These are all good reasons to be ready to move between prez-types. Next we explore how. How to hop, skip, and jump between prez-types. Which transitions work best and which transitions are riskiest.

How to **Combine Prez-types:** Hops, Skips and Jumps

◁ TIP

CHANGE
△ TIP 3

Combine as Presenting Partners

Form a presentation with a small team of presenters. Each presenter selects a different prez-type.

If you follow this tip, no presenter needs to juggle multiple delivery styles – each presenter selects one consistent prez-type. For example, you split the presentation into different sections, and share it out between two (or more) presenters. Each presenter selects a prez-type relevant to their content. This makes things very clear for you as you prepare the presentation and deliver the presentation. It makes things very clear for your audience as they listen.

It also allows people to play to their strengths. We often do this. When we present to potential new clients, occasions when we want to be at our very best, we talk to each other and decide who will be which prez-type. If we are sharing key information, for example, the catalogue of training courses that we offer, we will often "**double-down**" in partnership.

Richard selects the **sage prez-type.**

I am very happy being the geek – open to talk academically on what each course includes and why it is part of the curriculum. I eagerly answer any detailed question.

Kirstie selects the **student prez-type.**

I am very comfortable simplifying things for the client. Translating Richard's technical answers into real-world explanations that make the information easier to digest.

Each of us are helping the new client understand the training courses we offer. They get the impressive detail from Richard and the clearer simplicity from Kirstie. When they listen to Richard they are impressed. When they listen to Kirstie they are clear. A perfect combination.

Alternatively, when you **combine as presenting partners** you might use contrasting prez-types. In this scenario Richard communicates the impressive details by embodying the **sage prez-type**, while Kirstie concentrates on reassuring the client on how this will work for them by embodying the **caregiver prez-type**.

Richard selects the **sage prez-type.**

I am still happy to be the geek.

Kirstie selects the **caregiver prez-type.**

I am very comfortable guiding the client on what they can realistically achieve. Reassuring them how each course will help their people.

CHANGE △ TIP 4 | **Signpost Each Transition** | Signal to your audience that you are shifting to a new style. Do something that clearly indicates that you want them to change how they listen.

This is a fundamental tip for making a prez-type transition: signal the change to the audience.

If, instead, you do nothing to signal the transition, where there is no shift in your delivery, you are likely to confuse your audience. If you talk excitedly about all the fascinating new data in the research report (**explorer prez-type**) and then morph subtly to talk about our collective responsibility to take insights out of the research (**everyman prez-type**), your audience may fail to transition from "listening to learn" to "listening to take actions".

Ensure that you do something to signpost the change to your audience. This can be a short statement, or a stage move, or a pause in delivery. Take a moment to think about what sort of signal will work in your presentation.

For example, in our situation where you want to bridge between the explorer prez-type and the everyman prez-type, you might:

O Tell your audience.

> **E.g.** *"That completes our exploration of all the best insights from the research. Now I want to shift into a new section – I want to look at how we will work together to get the most value from these insights."*

O Make a "stage" move.

> **E.g.** If, while presenting as an explorer prez-type, you have been standing, sit down at the table to signal a change into an everyman prez-type.

O Switch to different visual aid.

> **E.g.** You have explored the insights using a range of PowerPoint slides. You close the computer and bring a flip chart forward as you shift into everyman prez-type.

O Pause and change tone.

> **E.g.** As you present in explorer prez-type you allow yourself to talk with increased energy and optimism. As you bridge you pause; you stop speaking for a number of seconds. As you begin in everyman prez-type you have calmed your delivery down, speaking in a collaborative and empathetic tone.

These transitions can be really powerful; they can re-establish focus from your audience and refresh their energy. Enjoy these moments. Make something of these shifts. Consciously find a way to signal that a transition is being made.

Different **Prez-type Transitions:** Hops, Skips and Jumps

Are all prez-type transitions created equally? Do some work better than others? Are some ideal for some scenarios? Are some wrought with danger? We are not going to get too deep into these questions in this book; instead, we offer you a few guiding principles.

Three Good Prez-type Combos: Hops, Skips, and Jumps

You have probably guessed this: how far you leap will affect how your audience responds. When you only hop a short distance (e.g. from **explorer prez-type** to **hero prez-type**), the impact on the audience is quite different from a huge jump across to the other side (e.g. from **explorer prez-type** to **everyman prez-type**).

Below we look at three valuable leaps: **hops**, **skips**, and **jumps**. Imagine you have started in the **magician prez-type**.

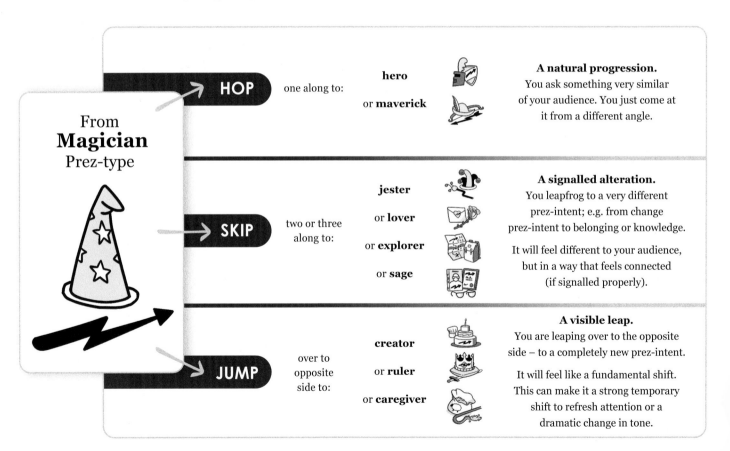

From Magician Prez-type

HOP one along to:
- hero
- or **maverick**

A natural progression.
You ask something very similar of your audience. You just come at it from a different angle.

SKIP two or three along to:
- jester
- or **lover**
- or **explorer**
- or **sage**

A signalled alteration.
You leapfrog to a very different prez-intent; e.g. from change prez-intent to belonging or knowledge.

It will feel different to your audience, but in a way that feels connected (if signalled properly).

JUMP over to opposite side to:
- creator
- or **ruler**
- or **caregiver**

A visible leap.
You are leaping over to the opposite side – to a completely new prez-intent.

It will feel like a fundamental shift. This can make it a strong temporary shift to refresh attention or a dramatic change in tone.

These moves feel very normal and intuitive. They are small steps in the type of presentation. Any shift in prez-type comes with challenges, but these will feel instinctive. You are asking very similar things of your audience – you're making a small alteration in the direction of your prez-intent.

This allows you to guide an audience. You start in the prez-type that fits with where they are, or where they want to be, and you step them in the direction that you want to take them.

Here are three examples.

Explorer to Sage
prez-type

Explorer: You enthusiastically explore the content. You have a sense of optimism for what you find along the way. You are researching what can be learnt and testing ideas. You present with a sense of adventure.

Hop to **Sage:** You start to review the information. You spotlight consistent themes. You set out specific theories and see if the evidence backs these up.

Ruler to Caregiver
prez-type

Ruler: You remind the audience of the targets that you have set them for the year. You summarise the priorities for the upcoming quarter, and lay out the expectations on them collectively and individually.

Hop to **Caregiver:** You return to the list of expectations, giving guidance for each one. You emphasise help and support available, and how it can be accessed.

Jester to Maverick
prez-type

Jester: You start with a fun activity: splitting the audience into teams and quizzing them on their memory of the "company vision" and the "company mission statement". You gently ridicule the teams for being so bad at recalling the language.

Hop to **Maverick:** You start to question the audience – if these are the values of the company, shouldn't we be able to name them? If they are the wrong values, shouldn't we be creating our own?

You can take a small number of hops. However, we would limit how many hops you make – if you make too many, you will make yourself, and your audience, dizzy!

"SKIP" = A Signalled Alteration

These are more obvious changes in direction. Like a sailing boat tacking left or gybing right. You are asking your audience to make a larger shift in how they should listen and respond to your presentation. If you were in **hero** prez-type, convincing your audience of the imperative to change course, you might skip over to **jester** prez-type to allay their fears.

These prez-type skips must be felt by the audience. If you are captaining a sailing dinghy and tack without warning your crew may end up swimming. You announce you are about to tack, and maybe warn them to duck before the boom swings over. When you skip prez-type, be the captain of your presentation ship – announce to all on board that the presentation is tacking onto a new direction.

Here are two examples.

Sage to **Hero** prez-type	**Ruler** to **Lover** prez-type
Sage: You carefully analyse the data for production across the quarter. You explain the significance of each set of information. Your focus is on the data slides, pulling out each vital insight.	**Ruler:** You clarify the work priorities for the team. You remind them of macro and micro goals. You state what is expected, by when, and by whom.
Slowly a consistent picture appears – there is a fault on the line.	You announce we are moving to monthly progress meetings. You brief them on who will set up and lead each meeting.
Skip to Hero: You step purposely to the centre of the stage, away from the screen. At the moment the issues are minor, but pretty soon the faults will multiply exponentially.	**Skip to Lover:** You make a noticeable change in tone. You acknowledge that this is challenging work. You remind the team of your admiration and respect for everything they do. They are the best people making up an elite team.
It is time for all hands on deck. We must identify where faults are so we can understand possible solutions. This has to be our only priority for the next week.	If there is anything they need – your door is always open. They just have to ask.

Prez-type "skips" can be hugely effective. They can also be the most challenging combinations. As you build your experience in prez-type combinations, these moves might be best done as presenting partners. Two presenters, each embodying one of the two prez-types. This keeps it really clear to the audience.

You make an about-turn to a prez-intent in the opposite direction. You may have started as a **magician** prez-type, amazing the audience with the technology, but you make a large jump over to **caregiver** prez-type to guide them through how to bring the technology to market. These transitions bring a dramatic change in focus for the audience. They can be incredibly powerful, but they should be handled with care.

These prez-type shifts should be utterly transparent to your audience as the change is so significant. This is no time for subtlety – make the jump clear.

Here are three examples.

Sage to Jester
prez-type

Sage: You are educating your audience on detailed shopper psychology principles. It is an interesting topic, but there are twenty-three separate tenets within the toolbox. The audience starts to tire.

Jump to **Jester:** Every five-to-ten minutes, you drop in a funny anecdote from real shopper research. Each emphasises a point you are making, but mostly the laughter gives everyone a mental break.

Caregiver to Magician
prez-type

Caregiver: You are leading a workshop to sketch out the marketing plan for the next twelve months. You guide the group through many topics, ready to step in with advice where needed.

Jump to **Magician:** Half-way through the session, you dramatically switch into a new presentation style. You announce that they have the foundations for a powerful plan. You highlight the amazing ideas that they have included. You confidently predict this plan will bring unprecedented business success.

Everyman to Explorer
prez-type

Everyman: You are describing the objectives for your presentation: to review the results of the yearly staff satisfaction survey. You emphasise our collective responsibility to learn from the analysis.

Jump to **Explorer:** You announce that we are ready to get into it. You have shifted your tone to one of adventure and excitement in things to be found.

Prez-type jumps make the most striking and impactful combinations. They should be used with care and attention. When you do use them, never make them a subtle shift: be bold with each jump.

Some prez-type combinations are ripe with danger; you will be sailing into choppy waters, with sharp rocks peeking out of the water, and hungry sharks on the prowl. We recommend you avoid them. These tricky transitions are ones that involve a shift of exactly four steps. They create sets of prez-type tricky trios. They are:

Travelling between any of two prez-types within the same trio is tricky; not impossible, but risky.

Why? In the case of magician, everyman, and student, each has an essence which another contradicts. The magician asserts a capability that no one else has – which is anathema to the essence of us all being equal (everyman). The magician also maintains that we cannot completely understand the power of the magic – which is contrary to the core of a student, who believes there is a simple explanation that we can each comprehend.

In the prez-type DO IT chapters, you will always find a section on the final page that explains the Tricky Transitions. Prez-type transitions that you are advised to avoid.

If you **absolutely need to make this type of transition**, say from magician to everyman, we recommend that you make it a combination of hops, skips, and jumps. For example, if you want to go from magician to everyman:

- ⭕ magician – hop to maverick – skip to everyman.
- ⭕ magician – jump to caregiver– hop to everyman.

There is an alternative, but this involves carefully using the 🌶 mild-intensity levels for each prez-type. For example, let's say you want to move from jester to ruler. This is a very tricky transition. It is hard to take someone seriously as a ruler, if five minutes ago they were cracking jokes.

You can make the move less treacherous by transitioning from a 🌶 mild-intensity variant of the prez-type. In each prez-type chapter there is a page of "Intensity of" prez-type. For example, the jester can be a 🌶 mild-intensity fool-jester or a 🌶🌶 medium-intensity funster-jester or a 🌶🌶🌶 hot-intensity merrymaker-jester. The ruler prez-type can be a 🌶 mild-intensity gatekeeper-ruler, or a 🌶🌶 medium-intensity maestro-ruler, or a 🌶🌶🌶 hot-intensity sovereign-ruler.

If you want to go from ruler to jester, move from 🌶 mild to 🌶🌶🌶 hot-intensity (e.g. gatekeeper-ruler to merrymaker-jester). Or move from 🌶🌶🌶 hot- to 🌶 mild-intensity (e.g. sovereign-ruler to fool-jester). If you feel you have mastered all of the other prez-type combinations, there is an abundance of interesting options available by varying intensity levels.

Uniquely **Yours**

Personalising a prez-type so it feels like home.

At the beginning of this book we shared the story of how Richard started out as a "Peter Snow" style of presenter. He was bouncing around with gleeful exuberance as he shared distilled market data to a supportive team. In the language of **The Prez Method**, he was presenting as a student prez-type.

However, Richard was presenting beyond a generic student prez-type; it was a much more personalised version of it. It was a performing style uniquely Richard, which he could amplify by turning up the essence of Peter Snow.

We then read about how Richard learned to shift into a more credible and wise style of presenter: "Gandalf". He would whisper "*I am Gandalf*" to himself and found he transformed into a more convincing and expert presenter. He was suddenly a sage prez-type.

However, Richard was presenting beyond a generic sage prez-type; it was a more personalised version of it. A version of sage imbued with all the delightful nuances of being "Galdalf-like".

Through this book we have described twelve fundamental presenter types. These come with standard names like "hero" and "explorer". These are great for becoming confident in using **The Prez Method**. These may lack the individuality you want – something that more fully includes the things that make you amazingly and uniquely you.

If that is the case, we encourage you to find your own names for each prez-type.

Your sage prez-type may be named something quite different: *The Deep Thinking Prof, or Gary The Geek*, or *Captain Brainbox*, or *Everything Einstein*. By crafting a name that resonates most with you, you are helping your subconscious live within the style.

What can help is to consider people who have inspired you in the past. People whose style of presenting you would like to replicate in some way.

They can be based on a real person. In the opening story, people observed that Richard presented like Peter Snow, and told him this. Richard was encouraged to work out why. Richard studied Peter Snow's amazing data presentations on BBC television and picked out the elements that he wanted to build more into his presenting style. Now, when Richard wants to bring an enthusiastic yet simplified understanding of something complicated, he switches on "Peter Snow" rather than "student".

These can be fictional people (played by real people). Richard was inspired by Sir Ian McKellen's amazing portrayal of the character Gandalf. Perhaps, you would prefer to harness Emma Watson's portrayal of Hermione Granger. Perhaps, you would prefer to embody a delivery of Benedict Cumberbatch as Sherlock Holmes. Let your love of stories in various forms help evolve each of your prez-types into something more vivid for you.

We are not suggesting you are aiming for an imitation of these people. That is a completely different skill. Your aim is always to ground your performance in an authentic version of you. A presentation that stays true to you and your values. But a little creative fun can help you shift faster and further.

For prez-types that you plan to use regularly, add your own details, your own quirks, to raise the delivery from a standard (and effective) prez-type into your own well-rounded prez-style.

Jackson is a Tlingit artist and master carver from Alaska.[38] He is best known for his exquisite totem poles. In describing the connection between his work and the ancient traditions of Tlingit art, he once said:

"There are standard elements of design, and you go from there to create a style that's identifiable as your own."

Yéil Yádi Nathan Jackson

This book offers you twelve different long-established elements of design for your presentations. It is time for you to create the presentation styles that are uniquely yours.

A Little More On **Archetypes**

Learning from psychology, marketing theory, and drama.

A cornerstone of this book is the idea that we can shift into any of twelve types of presenter from twelve classic archetypes. These archetypal presenter types then enable us to become more versatile presenters and encourage our audience to listen and respond in predefined ways. Through the chapters where we covered **The Prez Method** we chose not to go into much detail on why this happens. We kept to an explanation of how to use the process and hoped you would trust us on the why.

Across the next few pages we come back to the why. We dig a little deeper into why archetypes help us. We look at the value of archetypes from three different fields: from psychoanalysis, from marketing theory, and finally from drama. Within each field we consider the insights we can gather for why archetypes are such a powerful tool for us as presenters.

Field 1: Psychology

If Freud is the most famous name in psychoanalysis, Carl Jung is the second. Jung was not the first to use the term "archetype",[39] but Jung is the true father of how many of us use the term today. Here is how Jung described something as being "archetypal":

> *"An image can be considered archetypal when it can be shown to exist in the records of human history, in identical form and with the same meaning."*

Carl Jung defined a range of different archetypes, with names like "The Animus" and "The Hero". Carol S. Pearson took Jung's thinking and formalised the core set of twelve that we commonly use today.[40] We can understand archetypes as aspects of culture (art, drama, music, etc.) and society (talking, interacting, etc.) that humans create in consistent ways and importantly as aspects that humans respond to in consistent ways. For example, people consistently connect ideas around hope with words and images associated with light (sun, lighting a candle, etc.), whereas for ideas around despair they will use words and images associated with darkness (night, caves, etc.). Each culture will have a specific version, but the core essence, the archetype, is consistent.

Jung talked of three levels of consciousness: 1) *Consciousness* (what we perceive through our experience); 2) *Personal unconsciousness* (what affects us through past experience); and 3) *Collective unconsciousness* (the consistent ways we respond intuitively to present experiences regardless of our past experiences).[41]

The idea of archetypes sits within this third level – the insight that there is a *"collective unconsciousness"* shared by us all. There are common ways that humans have evolved to think and respond based on the consistent scenarios that we all face through our lives. We show caring for others in a number of consistent ways – a guiding hand, a firm yet considerate tone, a gentle push forward – and we recognise these actions when others care for us. We explore new experiences in similar ways – an optimism for what may be found, an anticipation to see round the next corner, the collection of souvenirs gathered along the journey – and those who inspire us to explore also inspire us to follow into new lands.

We act similarly and we respond similarly to certain images in *"identical form and with the same meaning"*.

What We Harvest as a Versatile Presenter

As presenters we focus a lot of attention on Jung's first area: the conscious needs of the audience. What do they know already? What are their experiences and expectations? What will interest them most? What will seem confusing to them? What will answer their questions?

We believe we should also give attention to Jung's third area: on the *"collective unconscious"* of the audience. How to signal to the audience how to think and how to listen. This is where the archetypes, or for us the prez-types, become invaluable. They allow us to tap into any audience's *"collective unconscious"* and to guide them to listen and respond in the way that we want.

Field 2: Marketing Theory

"The phenomenon [of archetype] is not about 'borrowing' meaning in an
ephemeral advertising campaign, but rather becoming a consistent
and enduring expression of meaning..."

Above is a quote from *"The Hero And The Outlaw"* by Mark and Pearson.[42] Inspired by the ideas of Jung, they formed a similar set of twelve archetypes. They laid these out in a thesis on how to use archetypes to create a *"consistent and enduring expression of meaning"* for a brand (a named product or service). That is, how to set the consistent elements of the brand's character, language and visual identity so that the brand feels clear and distinct in the eyes of the shopper or consumer. Those who are watching the brand's adverts, searching online for information about the brand, purchasing the brand, or using the brand, experience a consistent expression of the brand's language and visual form that also encourages the person to react to the brand in consistent ways.

A marketeer needs to protect and strengthen how consumers perceive their brand. They want their brand to feel distinct in the market – to have unique differences in relation to other brands. They want their brand to feel consistent with its heritage, cognisant of how consumers understand the brand from past messaging, and guide the shopper's perception of the brand going forward. They want the brand to intuitively communicate its place in the spectrum of other brands on offer.

Marketeers use archetypes to do this; as a way to set and articulate a consistent and enduring expression of brand meaning. They craft their brand identity through the language and imagery of archetypes.

For example, if you own the global brand of Volvo cars, you have spent decades nurturing the perception that a Volvo car is the safest car someone can buy. That the Volvo car is best placed to protect someone's family in a crash. Any marketing developed by Volvo needs to remember their heritage as a **caregiver** archetype. If you google for advertising from Volvo, you quickly see the archetypal caregiver language and imagery.

The marketeers are not "*borrowing meaning*" but rather setting firm rules for a "*consistent and enduring expression of meaning*". The consumer or shopper learns to recognise consistent representations in a form that they intuitively know how to respond to. The marketeer then adds unique elements authentic to the brand heritage and values. They mix the universal with the unique.

What We Harvest as a Versatile Presenter

We, as presenters, can use the same tool to set a style of presenting. A way to combine the universal (prez-type) with the unique (your personality and equity). A brand may be locked into a single heritage archetype but you are freer. As a presenter you can adapt to different scenarios and objectives. While still being true to your authentic self, your personal equity, you can pick a specific archetype style for your whole presentation, or move between archetype styles for each section of your presentation.

Field 3: Drama

Archetype: a standard character type seen in art and literature

Archetypes have existed as an idea in drama for hundreds of years. The playwrights of ancient times used consistent character types in their plays. In Roman plays, the "Senex" is the jealous old man, the "Miles Gloriosus" is the boastful soldier.[43] In medieval times, travelling players of commedia dell'arte included stock characters like the "Zanni" (where we get the modern word "zany") and "Pantalone".[44] Today, in the quirky theatre of UK pantomimes, we have set characters like the "Dame", the "Good Fairy", the "Villain", and the "Principal Boy".[45]

Through the use of consistent rules for staging, costuming, and character, an actor knew how to move, dress, and speak. For example, in a traditional UK pantomime, the Dame is a comedic character normally played by a man who wears large outlandish frocks (dresses). The Good Fairy enters from stage right (superstition says connected to Heaven) and the Villain enters from stage left (superstition says connected to Hell).

Signals like these help the audience to recognise who they are watching and how they are to respond. They know who to cheer (the Principal Boy), who to listen attentively to as they explain elements of the plot (the Good Fairy), who to laugh at (the Dame), and who to "booo" at (the Villain). The archetypal representations of instantly recognised stock characters help an audience focus on enjoying the story being told, confident in their understanding of who is who, and what each character is aiming to achieve.

What We Harvest as a Versatile Presenter

As a presenter, you do not want to be locked into stock characters. You should be free from the constraints of an unnatural stereotype. You need to be your authentic self. You need to be respectful of the situation. You want to be aligned with your content.

We can, however, notice that the audience loves to recognise these character types. They cheer the **hero**. They laugh at the **jester**. They listen attentively to the **sage**. The audience, in each case, relaxes as they know how to listen to, and how to react to, each character in the story.

The archetype becomes the way you signal to the audience the type of presenter you are being, which helps them understand the way they should listen and react.

Archetypes have been used for centuries as a way to differentiate between types of character. Jung articulated the consistent yet distinct character types in us all. Marketing theory tells us to use archetype language and imagery to create brand meaning. And playwrights and actors use archetypes to signal to an audience who is who within the story.

Each archetype, from whichever field, is built upon a set of unspoken "rules" on how to sound and how to move and how to look. We use these intuitive shortcuts to guide our hand as we craft our presentation. We use these same essences to shift how we talk and move as we present. Behind our practical tips for prez-types are all the established ideas within archetypes.

If you want to explore further, we list some of the books that have inspired us in the **bibliography** near the end of the book.

5 MORE?

Final Thoughts

There is so much more that we could have included in this book. For example: a deeper dive into structure options for each prez-type, explanations of different warm-up exercises, a full chapter on the origins of Jung's archetypes, an adventure into the theories of "actions" and "actioning" in drama, and so on. Earlier drafts of the book included chapters on these things and more. We realised we were creating an expensive door stop and not a practical workbook. So we stopped writing more.

However, if you want more, here are a few extra things in these final pages:

1) **Get in Contact:** how to get in touch with us.
2) **Access More Stuff:** some things we have added onto the website. Learn what to expect and how to get there.
3) **About Richard and Kirstie:** if you want to know a little more about the authors.
4) **Thanks to:** the people who supported us in innumerable ways to create this book.
5) **References and Bibliography:** where you can go to learn more from experts in connected fields.

Get in **Contact**

We would love to hear from you. Especially if you have questions or comments on the book.

To get to us, go through the website for the book:

www.versatilepresenter.com/contact

Access **More Stuff**

There are additional resources for you that are freely available through the website. These include:

O A printable PDF poster with all twelve prez-types laid out around the prez-intents.

O A template form to use as you prepare a presentation.

O Links to further articles on associated topics.

www.versatilepresenter.com/resources

About Richard and Kirstie

Richard and Kirstie have been training, coaching and consulting in presentation skills since they first met in 2003. Today, companies like Procter & Gamble, Carlsberg, Mattel and many more rely on their experience and expertise in all aspects of presentation skills training. Over the last twenty years they have trained many thousands of people in presentation skills, from large to small corporates, from charities and businesses, in over sixty countries across the main continents of the world. They continue to be fascinated by how everyone, from whatever background or generation, is struggling with the same set of presentation challenges.

Richard and Kirstie bring a perfect balance of two things: **geekiness** and **experience**. They are **geeky about all things associated with the science and art of presenting** (especially Richard). They are **experienced in the realities of delivering real presentations in real business situations** (especially Kirstie).

Geeky

They are nerdy in the many fascinating areas connected to presentation skills: how the **brain engages** with information; **behavioural sciences**; the principles of **visual design; story structures**.

They also mine from the arts: the principles of **stage craft**; the application of **improv theory**; and **vocal warm-up** processes employed by professional performers.

Nothing makes them happier than learning something new from a novel field of study that they can simplify and then use in their training.

Experienced

They have walked the walk. They have worked in classic commercial roles (**sales, marketing, external relations, insights**). They have presented business ideas in small rooms and they have delivered keynote speeches on large stages.

They have **led regional and global learning curricula**. They have crafted competency definitions, aligned learning priorities, and delivered global training interventions.

They have **significant stage experience**. From hosting professional conferences to coaching drama workshops, to acting and singing principal roles to audiences large and small.

They both live in the UK. Richard in the big northern city of Leeds and Kirstie in the small town of Emsworth on the south coast.

Thanks to

We want to thank those who inspired us to start this book. They include friends from the distant past. Jonathan Brown for challenging Richard in 2002 to stop complaining about the presentation skills in the company and to *Do something!* Neil Reed who in 2004 confidently told Richard that he would love to read a book written by him one day. Susie Oliver, Jason Ing, Bernhard Wessels and others, who trusted Kirstie and me to train them to run a new course called "Inspirational Presenter". Paul Smith, who showed that you could leave a huge Blue Chip company and start writing successful communication skills books.

They include friends who encouraged us to get started with the writing. Stef Parsons for being the most enthusiastic advocate right from the start. Mark Roberts for deciding to write his own excellent book (The Entrepreneur Within) at the same time, and so being the perfect learning partner as we all took our first tentative steps putting pen to paper.

We also want to thank the very many people who provided us with advice or read early drafts and gave such varied and surgical feedback on all that was wrong, while remaining consistently positive that it was worth us continuing down the path we had started. Anita Adams, Stephen Pascoe, Gareth Helm, Helen Tupper, Steve Phillips, Peter Yorke, Simon Michaelides, Sarah Case, Scott Pennwood, Marcella Edwards, John Cooper, Rebecca Barwick, Trudy Hills, Jamie Ward, Chantal Cornelius, David Shannon, Jenni Bowley, Guy Ousey, Lucy Coote, Alexandra Hawkes, Anna Austin, and Jasmine Caines.

Maybe the greatest thanks go to those who did the hard yards of proofreading every page. To be clear, any remaining errors are completely the fault of the authors. A huge thank you to Flo Toolan, Bridget Westmacott, Simone Gunn, and Louise Lupton for minimising our mistakes.

We could not have got anywhere without the expertise of those who know what it takes to write a non-fiction book. We are indebted to Debbie Jenkins at Intellectual Perspective Press, who has guided us patiently from our tangle of ideas through to this final book, and her team including Lisa de Caux, Jayr Cuario and Leanne Kelly. Andrea De Mauro was a constant calming presence in the later months, a successful writer of business books who found no question too basic and no idea too ridiculous.

Finally, our family. Claire and Greg and our kids who have put up with us hiding away in our offices writing when we could be doing something far more practical around the house (or fun on the water!).

References

01 – "Carl Jung's explanation of the 'collective unconscious' found in all of us." See: Carl Jung (translated by R.F.C. Hull), ***The Archetypes and the Collective Unconscious (Second Edition)***, 1968, Princeton University Press.

02 – "... personality profiles to help managers understand their working style". See: Merve Emre, ***What's Your Type?***, 2018, William Collins.

03 – "... marketing communications theory to help develop a unique and consistent equity". See: Mark & Pearson, ***The Hero And The Outlaw***, 2001, McGraw Hill.

04 – "... archetypes help screenwriters to craft distinct characters". See: Christopher Vogler, ***The Writer's Journey: Mythic Structure for Writers – Third Edition***, 2007, Michael Wiese Productions.

05 – "... archetypes help actors to morph into varied believable performances". See: Gunter Lösel, ***The Play Of Archetypes***, English Translation 2013, Lulu.com.

06 – "These are often books written by ex-salespeople." For example: Phillip Khan-Panni, ***Financial Times Making Business Presentations***, 2011, Pearson. A good book, but an example of a focus on selling/persuading.

07 – "It is 2001. The first of the *Lord of the Rings* trilogy of films, directed by Peter Jackson, is in cinemas." See: IMBD website. The Lord of the Rings: The Fellowship of the Ring. www.imdb.com/title/tt0120737/ (accessed September 2024).

08 – "Peter Snow is a well-known face on UK television." See: Tise Hahimagi, BFI Screen Online. BFI Screenonline: Snow, Peter (1938-) Biography (accessed September 2024).

09 – "Jamie is the Brand Director for SPAR UK". See: Spar UK main website. www.spar.co.uk (accessed September 2024). And LinkedIn page for Jamie. (14) Jamie Seymour | LinkedIn (accessed September 2024).

10 – "Paul Z Jackson". Author of ***The Inspirational Trainer: Making Your Training Flexible, Spontaneous and Creative***, 2001, Kogan Page. Quote from the 2002 version of "The Inspirational Presenter" training course.

11 - "The result is our audience wastes thinking time and focus on ascertaining what the presenter is trying to achieve." See: Jackson Hartley, achology.com. Attention's Blind Spot: The Impact of the Invisible Gorilla Experiment by Chabris and Simons. The Impact of the Invisible Gorilla Experiment Explained – Achology (accessed September 2024).

12 – "Our twelve prez-types are inspired by the archetypes proposed by Carl Jung". See: Carl Jung (translated by R.F.C. Hull), ***The Archetypes and the Collective Unconscious (Second Edition)***, 1968, Princeton University Press.

13 – "... personality profiling (e.g. MBTI)," See: Merve Emre, ***What's Your Type?***, 2018, William Collins.

14 – "... marketing theory," See: Mark & Pearson, ***The Hero And The Outlaw***, 2001, McGraw Hill.

15 – "... acting classes," See: Gunter Lösel, ***The Play Of Archetypes***, English Translation 2013, Lulu.com.

16 – "... screenwriting," See: Christopher Vogler, ***The Writer's Journey: Mythic Structure for Writers – Third Edition***, 2007, Michael Wiese Productions.

17 – "Actors talk of surrendering to their character's 'actions and transactions'". See: Jeff Zinn, ***The Existential Actor***, 2015, Smith & Kraus.

18 – "Typography is full of fascinating terms:" See: Monotype. Typography terms and definitions, https://www.monotype.com/resources/expertise/typography-terms-and-definitions (accessed September 2024).

19 – "The Royal Institution in London has maintained a similar calling, staging lectures for over 200 years" See: The Royal Institution – About Us. Official Page. https://www.rigb.org/about-us (accessed September 2024).

20 – "The nature documentaries of Sir David Attenborough." See: BBC iPlayer website. https://www.bbc.co.uk/iplayer/group/po3szck8 (accessed September 2024).

21 - "Those who are not shocked when they first come across quantum theory cannot possibly have understood it." See: Werner Heisenberg, *Physics & Beyond*, 1969 (in German) 1971 (in English). Heisenberg is quoting a conversation with Niels Bohr in June 1952.

22 – " Magic is not done, it is performed." See: John Cassidy and Michael Stroud, *The Klutz Book of Magic*, 1990, Klutz Press.

23 - "On January 9, 2007, at the Macworld conference in San Francisco, Steve Jobs stepped onto stage to unveil the new iPhone." See: Press release from Apple – Apple Reinvents The Phone With iPhone. Apple Newsroom, 9 January 2007. https://www.apple.com/uk/newsroom/2007/01/09Apple-Reinvents-the-Phone-with-iPhone/ (accessed September 2024)

24 - "Progress is impossible without change, and those who cannot change their minds cannot change anything." See: George Bernard Shaw, *Everybody's Political What's What*, 1944, Constable and Co.

25 – "Sheryl Sandberg's TED talk on 'Why we have too few women leaders'." See: TED Talks. Sheryl Sandberg, "Why we have too few female leaders. https://www.ted.com/talks/sheryl_sandberg_why_we_have_too_few_women_leaders? (accessed September 2024).

26 – "Tim Spector, professor of genetic epidemiology at King's College London, up-ending our understanding of nutrition." See: tim-spector.com. https://tim-spector.co.uk/mediacat/apperances-events/ (accessed September 2024).

27 – "Stephen Fry, at the Intelligence Squared event, debating the goodness of The Catholic Church." See: Intelligence Squared debate, 'The Catholic Church is a Force For Good In The World.' 2009. https://www.intelligencesquared.com/events/the-catholic-church-is-a-force-for-good-in-the-world/ (accessed September 2024).

28 – "Mhairi Black, in 2015, elected as the youngest UK MP since 1832, in her maiden speech…" See: BBC News website. 19 July 2015. https://www.bbc.co.uk/news/uk-scotland-scotland-politics-33585087 (accessed September 2024).

29 – Find "I got 99 problems… palsy is just one by Maysoon Zayid" on TED.com. See: TED Talks, TEDWomen 2013, Maysoon Zayid. https://www.ted.com/talks/maysoon_zayid_i_got_99_problems_palsy_is_just_one?subtitle=en (accessed September 2024).

30 – "Princess Diana's funeral was held in London in 1997. Her brother, Earl Spencer, delivered a moving tribute." See: Earl Spencer eulogy at funeral of Princess Diana, September 1997. BBC website. Clip from speech here: https://www.bbc.co.uk/programmes/po0wsvz0 (accessed September 2024). Full transcript here: https://www.bbc.co.uk/news/special/politics97/diana/spencerfull.html (accessed September 2024)

31 – "Tous pour un, un pour tous." See: Alexandre Dumas in collaboration with Auguste Maquet, *Les Trois Mousquetaires (The Three Musketeers)*, 1844. The famous French historical adventure novel.

32 – "We cannot predict the future, but we can invent it." See: Dennis Gabor, *Inventing The Future*, 1964, Penguin Books.

33 - "In the excellent TED Talk 'Your Elusive Creative Genius', Elizabeth Gilbert muses on the unrealistic expectations laid on artists to be geniuses." See: TED Talks, Elizabeth Gilbert, 'Your Elusive Creative Genius'. February 2009. TED.com. https://www.ted.com/talks/elizabeth_gilbert_your_elusive_creative_genius?subtitle=en (accessed September 2024)

34 – "For example, the Fully Charged YouTube channel ran a series on buying a first electric car." See: Maddie Moate, on Fully Charged Show. March 2020. https://fullycharged.show/episodes/maddie-goes-electric-supercut/ (accessed September 2024).

35 – "As we write this book in 2024, Generative AI large language models (LLMs) are exploding into our working lives." See: The Royal Institution – The Turing Lectures with Mike Wooldridge – 'What's the future for generative AI?'. December 2023. https://www.youtube.com/watch?v=b76gsOSkHB4 (accessed September 2024).

36 – "If you know any principles of behavioural psychology you may be well versed in the concept of "System 1 and System 2" (or sometimes described as "Brain 1 and Brain 2")." See: Daniel Kahneman, **Thinking, Fast And Slow**, 2011, Farrar, Straus and Giroux.

37 – "Actors learn to surrender to the role – to let their intuitive-self take more control." See: Jeff Zinn, **The Existential Actor**, 2015, Smith & Kraus.

38 – "Jackson is a Tlingit artist and master carver from Alaska." See: National Endowment for the Arts – National Heritage Fellowships – Nathan Jackson, 1995. https://www.arts.gov/honors/heritage/nathan-jackson (accessed September 2024). And Norman Jackson official website at https://www.normanjackson.com/ (accessed September 2024).

39 – "Jung was not the first to use the term "archetype"." See: Oxford English Dictionary – 'archetype – noun'. https://www.oed.com/dictionary/archetype_n?tl=true (accessed September 2024).

40 – "Carol S. Pearson took Jung's thinking and formalised the core set of twelve that we commonly use today." See: Carol S. Pearson, **Awakening the Heroes Within**, 2015, Harper One.

41 – "Jung talked of three levels of consciousness: 1) Consciousness (what we perceive through our experience); 2) Personal unconsciousness (what affects us through past experience); and 3) Collective unconsciousness (the consistent ways we respond intuitively to present experiences regardless of our past experiences)." See: Carl Jung (translated by R.F.C. Hull), **The Archetypes and the Collective Unconscious (Second Edition)**, Princeton University Press, 1968.

42 – "Above is a quote from "The Hero And The Outlaw" by Mark and Pearson." See: Mark & Pearson, **The Hero And The Outlaw**, 2001, McGraw Hill.

43 – "In Roman plays, the 'Senex' is the jealous old man, the 'Miles Gloriosus' is the boastful soldier." See: PBS Digital Studios – Crash Course Theatre. 'Roman Theater [sic] with Plautus, Terence, and Serneca'. 2018. https://www.pbs.org/video/roman-theater-with-plautus-terence-and-seneca-ujh8ca/ (accessed September 2024).

44 – "In medieval times, travelling players of commedia dell'arte included stock characters like the 'Zanni' (where we get the modern word 'zany') and 'Pantalone'." See: Richards, **Commedia Dell'arte: A Documentary History**, 1990, Wiley-Blackwell.

45 – "Today, in the quirky theatre of UK pantomimes, we have set characters like the 'Dame', the 'Good Fairy', the 'Villain', and the 'Principal Boy'." See: Victoria & Albert Museum, 'The Story Of Pantomime'. https://www.vam.ac.uk/articles/the-story-of-pantomime (accessed September 2024).

Bibliography

Jane Drake Brody, ***Acting, Archetypes, & Neuroscience***, 2016, Routledge. Brody connects three huge topic areas in a relatively short book. This means some areas miss the depth and breadth that you may want. However, her aim to explain the neuroscience behind key elements of acting and archetypes is very informative.

Joseph Campbell, ***The Hero With A Thousand Faces***, 1949, Princeton University Press. The classic text that brings together the insights of modern psychology with the deep exploration of mythology across cultures. Available in multiple editions.

Declan Donnellan, ***The Actor And The Target***, 2002, Nick Hern Books. A really excellent evaluation of the challenges of stage acting. Donnellan skilfully explains how important it is to focus the ways the actor is aiming to influence the other characters on stage (the target). This insight connects to our tenet that the presenter should focus on the responses of their target: the audience.

Hartwell & Chen, ***Archetypes In Branding, A Toolkit For Creatives And Strategists***, 2012, How Books. An inspiring book that articulates sixty different archetypes to be used in various spheres of work. On closer inspection we see the same twelve archetypes that Mark & Pearson use (see below); Hartwell & Chen have split each into five more granular archetypes.

André Jolles, ***Simple Forms***, 1958 (English translation 2017), Verso. Not for the faint hearted – this is a heavy read. However, it includes profound insights in the structures and principles of nine different literary forms.

Gunter Lösel, ***The Play Of Archetypes***, 2008 – English Translation 2013, Self-published. This looks at Campbell's articulation of Jung's eight original archetypes. It is especially strong in the areas of body language and movement. It is aimed at actors rather than presenters, but we can reinterpret some of his ideas for our world of business communications.

Mark & Pearson, ***The Hero And The Outlaw***, 2001, McGraw Hill. Mark & Pearson passionately advocate the use of archetype ideas as a way to define and portray brand meaning. They detail the same twelve archetypes as we describe in this book (we use some alternative names and there are differences in emphasis). They are describing the essence and representation of each archetype through the lens of marketing language, but we can reimagine their ideas in the discipline of presenting.

Martin & Marks, ***Messengers: Who We Listen To, Who We Don't, and Why***, 2019, Random House Business. Martin & Marks use their own list of types of communicators, so do not correlate directly into what we use. More of a general exploration of the impact of different styles of communicating rather than an explanation of how to use different styles.

Paul Smith, ***The 10 Great Stories Great Leaders Tell***, 2019, Simple Truths. Paul achieves the startling feat of summarising ten different types of story to tell in ten different management situations, and all in a book you could read on a short flight.

Anthony Stevens, ***Jung: A Short Very Short Introduction***, 2001, Oxford University Press. A good overview of Carl Jung's life, the early influence of Freud, and the break away from Freud to form his own distinct thinking, including the area of archetypes.

Christopher Vogler, ***The Writer's Journey: Mythic Structure for Writers – Third Edition***, 2007, Michael Wiese Productions. A very readable book exploring the structure of a classic story, heavily inspired by the work of J. Campbell. It includes vivid descriptions of the original eight archetypes put forward by Carl Jung.

Jeff Zinn, ***The Existential Actor***, 2015, Smith & Kraus. Zinn does an excellent job summarising some of the twentieth century's most successful methods for acting. He then advances his own core method: Shape, Action, Transaction, and Surrender. The first three connect in different ways to the steps of **The Prez Method**. His fourth area, "Surrender", is useful for anyone wanting to explore further our ☆ tip to "Concede to Succeed". To trust our instincts in the moment.

More Praise for the Book

Mark Given

Chief Marketing Officer at J Sainsbury's PLC
Fellow of the Marketing Society

"Improving your presenting capability is, for me, one of the most important career investments we each make. This book outlines a genuinely fresh approach that I hadn't seen before. It's a book and approach that helps regardless of the stage you are at, whether you are taking first steps or are already highly accomplished."

Stefanie Parsons

Managing Director Mizzouri GmbH

"I am incredulous that this level of innovation is possible in the crowded presentations space. Richard and Kirstie's book has me hooked and eager to experiment with my prez-intent and with one of the 12 prez-types, most of which I've never used such as the Everyman, the Explorer, or the Maverick. They outline credible theory, and practical DO IT guides and jump forward options which allow for application in just 20 minutes. If you enjoy presenting and think you're reasonably good at it, I urge you to buy this book."

Peter Yorke

Former Global Head of New Systems
Innovation, Nespresso

"Over 30 years in business, the biggest opportunity I saw was for people to communicate their thinking better. This book can unleash that hidden potential."

Jose Domingo Verdera

Pan-EMEA Marketing Director Mattel Inc.

"Great book! I had the pleasure to have very powerful and insightful conversations on Communication with Kirstie and Richard, which helped develop new skills, and this book is a great summary of all the various topics we discussed. I am sure it will be a great help for people wanting to explore these subjects."

Vincent Barnes

Tesco Global Vice-President,
Procter & Gamble

"What sets this book apart is the way Richard & Kirstie have created a simple but compelling structure to guide you towards becoming a better presenter. Keeping what is uniquely you, but unleashing your potential through a framework with countless examples!"

Adam Bishop

Marketing and Product Leader

"I love the passion and thoughtfulness that Richard and Kirstie have put into this book. They've found a gorgeous way to perfectly mix the art and science of presenting together. The thinking and the frameworks here will work for both seasoned pros and newcomers to presenting (and everyone in between). Most importantly, this book injects fun, craft and inspiration into how you'll think about your next presentation."

Glossary of Key Terms

The Prez Method™   The four-step process which will help design and deliver a presentation. The first two steps deal with strategy: (1) SET: what you intend to achieve from your presentation; and (2) SELECT: what type of presenter you will centre your presentation around. The final two steps deal with execution: (3) SHARPEN: choices you make to tailor your presentation design; and (4) SHIFT: how you will adapt your style to embody the type of presenter you have chosen.

Prez-intent   The statement of your intention; what you want your audience to do as a result of your presentation. There are four directions that your prez-intent may take: knowledge (you want your audience to increase their understanding in a topic); change (you want your audience to change their viewpoint or perspective); belonging (you want your audience to feel trust in you, themselves, or the team); and actions (you want your audience to complete a sequence of steps or actions).

Prez-type   The type of presentation that you will design and deliver. There are twelve prez-types, each inspired by twelve well-known archetypes. The prez-type acts as a creative seed, guiding the form of your presentation and the way you perform your presentation. The prez-type then encourages your audience to listen and respond in a particular way. The twelve primary prez-types and their key essence are shown on the next page.

Prez-type intensity   The intensity of the prez-type that you use. Each of the twelve prez-types can vary in their strength, from a very muted form to a heightened form. For example, a maverick can be a mild-intensity version: an outsider-maverick who asks probing questions only. Or a maverick can be a medium-intensity version: a reformer-maverick who looks to drive change from within. Or a maverick can be a hot-intensity version: a revolutionary-maverick who eagerly smashes existing habits and practices in the quest to form a completely new reality.

Prez-style   The version of you that you choose to deliver your presentation. This is the version of you, your authentic self, inspired by the choices you have made as you progress through The Prez Method. Ultimately this is what the audience will see, and respond to.

hero

...you convey a compelling cause and inspire commitment

magician

...you attest that the impossible is now possible

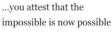

explorer

...you drive curiosity and chart discovery

maverick

...you provoke dissatisfaction in the status quo

sage

...you evaluate and then express expertise

jester

...you connect people by bringing the fun!

...you digest the information to teach the layperson

student

lover

...you make people feel valued and valuable

...you eagerly demonstrate the usefulness of your creation

creator

...you unify behind a common purpose and a collective responsibility

everyman

...you establish direction and direct action

ruler

caregiver

...you guide progress and provide guardrails

Copyright

Book Coach: Debbie Jenkins

Illustrations: Richard Pascoe and John Cooper

Inside Design: Richard Pascoe and Leanne Kelly

Cover: Richard Pascoe and Jayr Cuario

Editor: Lisa de Caux

Personal **Notes**

Personal **Notes**

Personal Notes

Personal **Notes**

BV - #0074 - 240225 - C178 - 216/216/17 - PB - 9781908770776 - Gloss Lamination